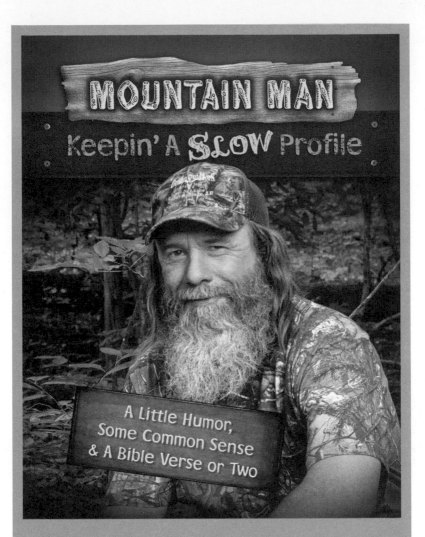

MOUNTAIN MAN

Keepin' A SLOW Profile

A Little Humor,
Some Common Sense
& A Bible Verse or Two

BroadStreet
PUBLISHING

BroadStreet Publishing Group
Racine, Wisconsin, USA
www.broadstreetpublishing.com

MOUNTAIN MAN: Keepin' a Slow Profile

ISBN-13: 978-1-4245-4939-9 (print book)
ISBN-13: 978-1-4245-4952-8 (e-book)

Disclaimer from the author: This is my story and the book is true and as accurate as I can remember. The information and advice provided in this book is designed to provide entertaining and helpful information on the subjects discussed. This book is not meant to be used, nor should it be used, to diagnose or treat any condition that requires professional assistance. Please consult a professional as needed. The author or publisher is not responsible for actions taken as the result of reading this book. We sincerely hope you enjoy the book and are encouraged to walk on the trail God has for you.

All Scripture is taken from the New King James Version®. Copyright © 1982 by Thomas Nelson, Inc. Used by permission.

Design by Garborg Design Works, Inc. at www.garborgdesign.com
Typesetting by Katherine Lloyd, www.TheDESKonline.com

Stock or custom editions of BroadStreet Publishing titles may be purchased in bulk for educational, business, ministry, fundraising, or sales promotional use. For information, please e-mail info@broadstreetpublishing.com.

Printed in China

CONTENTS

PART THREE: A LITTLE MORE ABOUT MOUNTAIN MAN

I met Mountain Man after having a conversation with my brother Willie about finding an air conditioner man to work on my system. I remember Willie telling me that Mountain Man could fix the problem, but if I chose to have a conversation with him during the process, I would need to get comfortable. Of course I had no idea what Willie meant until I actually met Mountain Man.

Mountain Man and I became friends and we had many talks about hunting, family, and life in general. At some point in our friendship, Mountain Man asked me if I would study the Bible with him. I told him to come anytime to the duck call shop at Duck Commander and we could talk. I have to admit that the idea of having Mountain Man in the duck call shop was a sure-fire way of breaking up the monotony of building duck calls. However, the duck call shop is a good, relaxed setting to reflect on things that really matter.

Mountain Man started coming to the shop almost on a daily basis in between his heating and air-conditioning jobs, and he had many questions about the Bible, relationships, and faith in God. The Robertson family welcomed Mountain Man into our homes and he started coming to church with us on a weekly basis.

After about a year, Mountain Man called me up on the phone and I could tell he was a bit emotional. It took him a few minutes longer than normal to inform me he wanted to surrender to Christ and asked me if I would baptize him. After a film shoot a few days later, I baptized him at our church. It was an awesome moment for both of us and his actions say a lot about a man being open to change his direction in life.

It wasn't that Mountain Man hadn't been a religious man up to this point, but he wanted to be sure about his relationship with God. He had come to realize the grace of God on a cross and the power of the resurrection for him personally.

One of the questions I get asked a lot as I travel throughout the country is, "Does Mountain Man really talk like that?" My answer is always, "Yeeeeeeeeeeeeeeeessss," in my best Mountain Man imitated voice.

In the episode where I attempted to imitate Mountain Man for the first time, I also made a reference about Han Solo trying to understand Chewbacca. After Mountain Man watched the episode of the show, he was a bit concerned that it might be embarrassing for him to go out in public. I was also baffled to learn he had never seen the movie *Star Wars*. I told him we were only making fun of him because we cared about him and that he needed to immediately go and rent *Star Wars* from the movie house. It led to a good discussion about imitation being the best form of flattery. I could tell he wasn't too sure about that, but after a while he thanked me for "making him famous."

It was all in good fun, but through this experience we talked about having thick skin on little stuff and having your heart right when it comes to the big stuff like faith, family, and friendships. Mountain Man has become one of the more likable people on *Duck Dynasty* because he's willing to laugh at himself and fire back at my family in view of our quirks.

The bottom line is that our faith in Christ gives us opportunities for new beginnings and second chances. When you're forgiven and have hope in life after the grave, it gives you a peace in life that keeps you from taking yourself too seriously with the little things. Mountain Man has found a peace in Christ that has given him a platform to try and help others. I am proud that he has chosen to write a book to try and inspire others to do great things. Sit back and get comfortable, and may faith, hope, and love flourish in your life.

—Jase Robertson
Author of *Good Call: Reflections on Faith, Family and Fowl*

Read at Your Own Speed

Since my first appearance on *Duck Dynasty*, people are curious to know if I really talk this slow. W e l l , y e s I d o. But the good news is that you can read this book as fast as you want. We'll just see if I get to do the audio version.

I'm really excited to share my story with you. I think I had a special childhood and young-adult life, filled with some funny stories that shaped how I became Mountain Man. I'm also going to share some important lessons I've learned along the way so that you can keep a slow profile and make the most of the life the good Lord has given to you.

So sit on down, relax a bit, and enjoy the book.

PART ONE

MOUNTAIN MAN'S STORY

1

It's Okay to Be Different

On October 2, 1957, in Winnsboro, Louisiana, Frank and Ruth Guraedy (pronounced *jer-AH-dee*) welcomed a son into the world. They named him Tim. His sister, Lynn, was three and a half, and his brother, Bill, was two and a half. I was the new baby. Mountain Baby. And now I'm Mountain Man.

My daddy worked for a gas pipeline company in Extension, Louisiana. The company provided a house for us that stood in a row next to all the other company houses.

Across the cotton field lived our neighbors Ordy Mae and Red and about seventeen kids. Seriously, they had a big family. My daddy made a dollar or so an hour, which wasn't much, but sometimes we would need some help around the house. So Ordy Mae would come clean for us. If my parents went to town, they'd take my brother and sister and leave me with Ordy Mae. She loved little Tim.

I remember Ordy Mae as a large, caring woman with a

rag wrapped around her head. She'd rock me to sleep on the porch and say, "I just wish little Tim was mine. I love him to death." As we outgrew our clothes, we gave them to Ordy Mae because she had so many kids to care for. They were the best of kids.

My earliest memories are of catching big red crawfish with a string and some bacon. (By the way, if you want to see the best way to eat crawfish, check out my video on YouTube. Emm hmmm. They're really good.) Sometimes Ordy Mae's kids would come across the field and through the barbed wire fence to play with us. One of the boys was about my age—three years old—and had come over to play. We kids were always barefooted, just running around in our shorts. I had just grabbed my first crawfish. I was scared of their pincers, but my brother and sister had showed me how to pick them up without getting pinched. I was so proud of myself. The crawfish was huge, red, and mean looking. I was so excited to show him my crawfish. As soon as he saw what I was holding, his eyes got as big as silver dollars and he took off running across the cotton field so fast you could see the dust fly all the way to his house.

Minnesota

My daddy worked hard and also went to school to study compressor engines, which were the size of a large family room. He was determined to learn and his company sent him to

Hallock, Minnesota. I was three and we headed to a small town about twenty-five miles from the Canadian border.

The people were different. The land was vast and flat and winters were cold. Beautiful woods and clear lakes surrounded us. We played in the cemetery for fun and threw acorns at each other, and Daddy spent time teaching us how to fish.

Most kids have their favorite toys scattered around the living room—maybe superhero action figures or Legos. My daddy's shotgun sat in the corner and had my full attention. Of course it was empty with no bullets. He had them all hid. But my mama says I would stare at that gun for hours. Daddy showed me his pistol too, also with no bullets. I held it and stared at it. I just loved the pistol and the shotgun.

I got a BB gun and started to learn to shoot when I was about four. My dad set up a target in the basement that had little ducks going in circles. At four years old I could outshoot my brother and sister. I hit the target just about every time, which surprised my dad. I'd just laugh and keep shooting.

My dad turned us loose in the yard with the BB gun or our homemade slingshots. There wasn't a bird, chipmunk, acorn, or soda pop can that was safe. Daddy couldn't keep enough BBs in the house. I'd either be shooting at the target in the basement, roaming through the cemetery, or walking through the woods at the end of the street shooting everything I could shoot.

We'd climb way up to the top of oak trees and swing off

the limbs like squirrels. It was just our nature. Mama said I was wiry and was always trying to climb something. We had lots of time for fun in the summer because that far north it didn't get dark until close to eleven. When we heard Daddy's loud whistle, we knew it was time to come in. And we'd come on in.

In winter we went ice fishing and ice skating, and played hockey with sticks and a rock. I fell through the ice a time or two. The water wasn't very deep, but it was wet and cold! By the time I'd get back to the house, my clothes were frozen stiff.

We lived in Minnesota for five and a half years. I talked then like I do now—real slow with a southern accent—so kids made fun of me. When I started school, teachers would say, "It's *on*, not *own*." Or "Say *off*, not *awf*." I couldn't make the change. Thankfully after a while everyone got tired of making fun of me and I made some good friends and had a lot of fun.

The school administration wanted to hold me back from going into the second grade because I was too small. Mama didn't go for that, so I went on into the second grade. My favorite subjects were math and science and I was a good listener.

We all loved going to the theater. The show always started with a cartoon. I watched the cartoon, but was too young to understand the movie. I just enjoyed eating popcorn and drinking soda pop. Often Mama would look over to my seat and I'd be gone. My head would pop up four rows away from where they were sitting and I'd hear, "Get back here, boy. Quit crawling underneath the chairs."

When I was about six, I received another gift from Daddy: his US Air Force knife. I thought I was really hunting then. My dad, my brother, and I often went to a beautiful place called Lake of the Woods. The city is known as the walleye capital of the world. I had my BB gun and that knife, which dangled freely down the whole side of my leg.

I love the pull of the fish. I was amazed at how strong they grip the water so they don't come out. I caught my first fish on Lake Bronson. I caught a yellow perch on a cane pole. I loved to watch the float go under when the fish would bite and then feel the pull of the fish when it was time to reel it in.

I know this book is about keepin' a slow profile, but I want you to know that you can keep a slow profile and still catch fish fast. I talk slow and move slow, but that's when I speed up a little—when the fish are fighting. Growing up I'd have to pull the fish out quickly and recast before my brother or sister could drop their lines into my spot.

Bill and I were good friends growing up. When we fought, we never hit each other with our fists even though we probably felt like it a time or two. We'd just wrastle (that's how you say *wrestle* in the South). In those days our adventures covered a lot of woods, creeks, and lakes—including many frozen lakes during the long winters.

Tennessee

Just after Christmas when I was nine years old and in the third grade, my daddy got transferred and we moved to Portland, Tennessee. Portland was real small at that time with just one stoplight. Now when I go for a visit, it's easy to get lost.

Shortly after we arrived in Portland I got my first real gun—a .410 single barrel bolt action shotgun. Some kids sleep with teddy bears; I slept with my shotgun. That's the truth. Every time I got a new gun I slept with it. I didn't name my guns like some people do. But I was so proud of that gun.

The first thing I shot was a big bobwhite quail sitting on a fencepost. My uncle had come into town and we were all out riding around in the car. My uncle suddenly called out, "Stop and let Tim shoot that bobwhite quail off that fencepost."

My brother and sister where there and said, "Tim can't hit that."

I was like an old bird dog with my tongue hanging out. I was still really small, but got up out of the back seat and took aim. The sight bead went back and forth and around. When it got right on target, I pulled the trigger. *Boom*, there it went. I said, "I told you I'd get him!"

They couldn't believe it. "He got him! He got him!"

I ran over and got the giant quail and brought him back to the car. I was amazed. I had done killed me something, and it was good to eat.

My uncle said, "You'd better put that bird under the seat, Tim. It ain't quail season. You're going to get arrested."

I was scared to death and stuck it up under the seat. I didn't know whether it was the season or not. But Daddy cleaned it and we ate it. Emm hmmm. Delicious.

Then I started squirrel hunting. My first kill was a memorable one. I saw a squirrel run up a tree, and I guess I scared it so bad that it peed on me—right in my eye. So I retaliated and shot the squirrel. Daddy laughed, laughed, and laughed some more about that.

I really took to hunting. The first year my dad would clean the squirrels. He showed me what to do and I watched. By the second year he let me go out and hunt by myself. Sometimes my brother came with me, but I often went out alone because he preferred to fish.

The first time I came home with some squirrels I said, "Daddy, come on, clean these squirrels."

He said, "Son, I showed you how. Go out there and clean them."

So I did just like he said. First you grab the squirrel by the tail and flip it over so you're looking at its rear end. Next cut through the bone at the base of the tail, but not through the skin on the other side. Put your foot on the tail, grab the hind legs and pull the skin as far as you can pull. Then you can reach up under the belly side and pull the hide up over the shoulders. Then whack all that skin and his head off. My daddy always said, "Make sure you don't pull the tail off and you'll be all right."

Daddy told me to skin all the squirrels first and then gut

them. That kept the fur off the meat as much as possible. I felt like I had grown into a man at an early age, learning to kill and clean on my own. It didn't bother me to do it; it was a natural instinct to me and I enjoyed it.

When we weren't hunting, we would run in the woods, swing on vines, and find our way through a nearby cave. I walked through a cave with nothing more than a kerosene lantern. The others carried flashlights. The cave was about a mile long. When we got to the exit the first time we worked our way through the cave, everyone wanted to walk back to the car outside the cave.

I said, "Well, I'm going back through the cave."

"No, Tim, you're crazy."

"Yeah, I'll see y'all when y'all get over there. It's quicker to go through the cave." And I went through that cave with that kerosene lantern by myself and beat them back. If the lantern had gone out, I wouldn't have been able to see a thing since there's usually no light in a cave. That would have been hard since we had to duck while walking and watch for the creek that ran all the way through it. But I was always pretty brave about doing things. Gutsy, I guess you could say.

I loved the adventurous outdoors. Daddy bought us a little old Honda P50 and we loved to ride it out into the country. My brother and I covered a lot of territory—a lot of woods, a lot of lakes, a lot of creeks. We stomped out a lot of rabbits, squirrel, and fish. My brother says I was a competitor, always wanting to catch more fish than he did.

I learned to frog hunt at night when I was about ten. You only needed to stop and listen to hear them frogs bellowing at night, and we'd go straight to that pond. If you've never gone frog hunting, the best time to go out is when there's hardly any moonlight. You shine the flashlight into their eyes and sneak up on them quietly. When you get close enough, you stick them in the back with a gig that's on the end of a long stick. A gig is like a mini three-pronged pitchfork with fishhook barbs on the end. After you stick the frog, you yank it off the barbs and put it in a burlap sack.

One time I spent the night with a boy named Kerry. We decided to go out frog hunting and were supposed to be out only a few hours. It was well past midnight and we hadn't returned. After catching twenty-one frogs, we started walking back across the field to Kerry's house.

We could see that every light was on outside his house. As we got closer, I saw Daddy's company car sitting next to the house. We got a little closer and saw both sets of our parents standing there looking at us. I said, "I guess we're in trouble."

Kerry said, "What time is it?"

I said, "I don't know. Ain't got no watch." And boy, the closer we got, the meaner they looked.

The first thing I heard my daddy say was, "Here they come. I knew they'd come back. They probably got a sack full of frogs." My dad always had total confidence in me that I was going to return. He knew that I was born to hunt, fish, catch frogs, and run through the woods.

Mama was a little upset. But I think that Kerry's mama and daddy lit into him like all get out. Daddy said, "Well, you boys ought to let them know earlier when you're coming in." Daddy was kind of lenient about it. But Kerry's parents had already called the civil defense. Kerry got grounded, but Daddy and I just ate the frog legs.

I have lots of other great stories growing up, but I'll save some for later. I graduated from high school in Portland and went to Volunteer State Community College in Gallatin for two years. After college I started doing electrical work, working with some real Tennessee hillbillies. They were rough-collared redneck boys, and we worked hard.

During this time my dad got another transfer and headed north to Indiana. They lived in Terre Haute and Daddy drove to Paris, Illinois, each day for work. I stayed behind and was allowed to live in the company house. My brother had left to study in Texas and my sister was studying in Louisiana. So I had a job, a car, and a three-bedroom house all to myself.

Indiana

My daddy's company had given him the house in Tennessee as a part of a work deal, and he eventually decided to sell it. He said, "Well, Tim, why don't you come up here to Terre Haute? Your cousin Richard is doing heating and air-conditioning work. He makes good money. And your uncle

James, he makes good money. I'll send you to air-conditioning and refrigeration school. You come up here and you can stay with us."

So I moved to Indiana, got a job working at a gas station, and started school at Indiana Vocational Technical College, now called Ivy Tech. The first day of school I walked into a classroom filled with a bunch of Hoosiers. The teacher was a US Army drill sergeant veteran. We went around the room to introduce ourselves.

One said, "Hi, I'm so and so and I'm from Clinton."

Or "Hello, I'm from Terre Haute."

Or "Hey, I'm from right across the line in Illinois."

Then they got to me. "My name is Tim Guraedy. I'm from Tennessee."

The whole classroom busted out laughing. I guess they weren't expecting to hear my voice the way it is. One guy was laughing so hard he had to hurry to the bathroom so he wouldn't wet himself. The teacher said, "I'm right behind you!"

After that, everybody wanted to be my friend because I was different. All them Hoosiers and I got to be good friends. We did a lot of hunting together. The company my dad was in charge of had oil fields and some of the land had wooded hills and soybeans in the flats. And there were lots of deer. This is when I really got into deer hunting. I killed a nine-point buck the first year there. I was so proud of it and have had buck fever ever since.

Louisiana

After finishing school I had a hard time finding a good job in the area. My brother was living just outside New Orleans and told me there was some good work down there. So Mama and I drove down to see him and I immediately found a job doing heating and air-conditioning. Most of my work was in New Orleans, but I lived in Violet with my brother. He was single and I was single and we shared an apartment. I also learned to make metal ducting, installing it residentially and commercially. I got pretty good at the installation even though I had been trained in school to repair the equipment.

Back to Indiana

About a year later, I was in a bad wreck. I hit a telephone pole with a small truck and broke my nose and my left arm, busted some ribs, and got a bunch of stitches in my head. Since I couldn't work with a cast, my mom and dad flew me back to Terre Haute to stay with them. That was the first time I flew in an airplane. The timing was perfect; it was deer season again. Thankfully I could still shoot with a cast.

I remembered where I had killed that nine-point buck and returned to the same spot with a buddy of mine. I somehow managed to climb the tree with my broken arm and kill an eight-point buck. It was amazing.

I'll never forget field dressing that deer while my friend was watching me. He was turning whiter by the minute.

While I was skinning the deer, I cut too deep and hit the belly. It went *poof*, releasing the gas, and some of the guts flew out and landed on his face…right on his bottom lip. I looked over at him and he threw up.

That deer must have weighed one hundred ninety pounds. It took every bit of our strength to drag the body up and down those fields to get out of the woods. I don't think that old boy went hunting with me again. But we did cook it up and enjoyed a good meal. I was always good at cooking wild game—thanks to Mama showing me how to prepare the meat.

The arm break was pretty bad and took a good six months to heal. I tried to get another job back down in Louisiana, but ended staying in Terre Haute for about three and a half years.

Returning to Tennessee

I decided that I needed to go to Nashville to find work. I found a good job working for an air-conditioning-refrigeration company for about a year. About this time Daddy retired. I thought for sure he would move back to Tennessee. But no, he went straight back to West Monroe, Louisiana, and that's where he and my mama have been ever since.

I worked a while in Tennessee, but I got to missing my parents. So about twenty-five years ago I moved back to West Monroe. I told them, "I'm going to come live in the same town y'all are in." I wasn't married and had no ties, so I moved back to be around my family and do air-conditioning work.

During this time I got married and had a son. When Jonathan was about six months old, my dad saw an advertisement in the paper for a position at Popeyes. I didn't know it, but my dad wrote up a resume for me and sent it in. The next thing I knew this guy called me and said, "Hey, Tim, I love the application you sent us. I don't even want to interview anybody else." He told me to meet him at a little restaurant where he conducted his meetings. He said, "You'll know who I am. I'm the guy with all the tattoos and will be the meanest-looking, biggest, furriest guy there."

Sure enough. I opened up the door and found him in a second. He was very nice and a Vietnam vet. He said, "You're the man I want."

I said, "Well, what'll I be doing?"

He said, "You'll be working on cooking equipment, freezers, coolers, ice machines, mixers."

"Man, I don't know. I've never worked on that."

"You'll do just fine. You've been to school and if you can learn refrigeration and air-conditioning, that's most of it. The rest is easy. If you have any problems, call me."

So I worked at Popeyes for eleven and a half years and ate chicken every day. It was free, and I was proud to eat it. I had eight restaurants to service and was the only guy who could fix everything. If I had a problem, my boss had a unique way of making things real simple on the phone. He could even tell me the part that I'd need, including the part number. I called him every now and then, but for the most part I just caught on. I did a great job and they really liked me.

My son was almost twelve when I left Popeyes. To tell the truth, I got fired from Popeyes for dragging a deer into a restaurant's freezer.

The company that hired me gave me a company truck just to ride around in. I did such a good job that more than once the boss said, "Hey, you got everything caught up?"

I said, "Yeah."

"Well, ain't it deer season?"

"Yeah."

"Well, you'd better go deer hunting."

So off I went. I was appreciated that much.

One night I was out hunting with my son, Jonathan. We got ourselves a deer, but I also got a thorn in my eye. I was walking deep in the woods when I stumbled into a briar vine. The thorns went in one eye, but tears were running from both of my eyes. I could hardly see and Jonathan wasn't around to help me. So I called him on my walkie-talkie and told him to go get some help. He was hunting near the truck, put a pillow under his rear end so he could see over the dashboard, and drove down the gravel roads to the checkpoint station while pulling a four-wheeler on the trailer. The game warden was surprised to see this little guy climb out of the truck. They all knew me because I was a regular. He got the sheriff out there to holler for me and help me back to the truck. Then Jonathan drove me all the way from Union Parish back to our home in West Monroe. He was always a good little driver.

I didn't have the energy that night to clean the deer we had killed, so I dragged the deer into a big Popeyes' freezer so it wouldn't spoil and we could eat it later. The company had been making changes that I wasn't super happy about, so I probably didn't care too much about the consequences if I was caught. They found the deer and fired me. But by this time I was ready to get another job.

I worked for a few other air-conditioning companies. One of them fired me for being too slow. Then I worked for some laid-back country rednecks like me. We worked real hard during the summer. During the winter things slacked up so they said, "Well, you like to deer hunt, don't you?"

I said, "Yeah, yeah, yeah."

They said, "We're going to have to lay you off and you'll have plenty of time to hunt." They just couldn't afford to pay another hand, so that's the way it was.

I said, "I've got some money saved up so it'll be okay."

But the savings didn't last too long having a kid and a wife. So I had to get another job. I worked for a few other companies. I always found it amusing when they would read through my application and work history: "Volunteer State, Ivy Tech, electrical work, school of air-conditioning, Popeyes…" Then they read, "Fired for dragging a deer into the freezer." That was the best part. I couldn't wait for them to get to it.

They asked me, "Did you really do that?"

"Yeah, I did."

Every one of them always replied, "Well, that ain't no reason to fire a man."

I said, "Well, that's why they fired me. Check it out."

"Well, you're hired. We all love your application."

I always took the time to do a good job. I'm a little slow, but no one has to come back behind me and redo my work. For installation, if you don't do it right the first time, you're going to have to do it again. I was trained to do it the right way or else. If you tell people you're going to do a good job, you need to give them a good day's work.

I was also known for my honesty. Employees at Popeyes left me around the money, knowing that I wouldn't steal. I was always very professional and wouldn't use profanity in front of customers. I've always frowned on the use of profanity. If I was working with them, I'd say, "You can't talk like that around these people. It's not godly and it's not professional."

I was always very professional and I always listened. A lot of times when I went to people's houses, I would meet someone who didn't get out much to talk to anybody. I took the time to talk with them and it would slow me up. Maybe their kids lived a long way off, so I'd talk to them. If the company wanted to fire me for doing that, then so be it. I felt the smile on their faces meant more to me than having a hurry-up-and-get-the-job-done attitude. That's just the way I am.

I guess that's why I wasn't meant to do air-conditioning work for the rest of my life. I've always thought there was something else I needed to be doing. Years ago my daddy said, "I think one day you might be a preacher."

I just replied, "I don't know, Daddy. Do they make money?"

I finally got tired of working hard crawling around in hot, hot attics and coming out looking like a sheep from the blown insulation sticking to my sweaty skin. I thought, *How many years have I been doing this? Why don't I just start something on my own? I know enough people, and people like me.* I was always a favorite at the supply houses and got along with everybody because I would just bring laughter into our work environment. I love laughter, and I love to make people laugh.

So I got into business on my own. I never advertised and got all the business I needed by word of mouth.

How I Met Willie Robertson

One day I got a call from Willie's housekeeper's husband saying, "Willie Robertson wants you to work on his air conditioner."

I said, "What? Who is Willie Robertson?"

"Buck Commander."

"Buck Commander? Well, okay."

Then Willie's housekeeper called, "Willie Robertson wants you to work on his air conditioner. He's going to call you."

I said, "Okay."

A good friend of Willie's housekeeper first gave me the name Mountain Man. Marty called me Mountain Man because I grew up in the hills of Tennessee and was always in the woods. The name stuck and now most everyone calls me Mountain Man.

So when Willie called me, he said, "Hey, Mountain Man."

I said, "Hey."

He said, "This is Buck Commander."

I said, "Buck Commander?"

"Yes, Willie Robertson."

I said, "Willie Robertson?"

"Duck Commander, you heard of him? I'm Buck Commander."

"Oh, you're Phil's boy."

"Yeah, yeah. I need you to work on my air conditioner."

So I headed out to his place and we chatted a bit. He was a really nice guy. He'd had people work on his air-conditioning, but they couldn't fix it right and charged him an arm and a leg. I assured him I would do the job right and I would charge a fair price.

I noticed Willie liked to hunt and fish. I'd heard of his daddy, but had not met Willie. His oldest son, John Luke, was there. He was little bitty fellow back then. I got to talking to him and he laughed at all my crazy stories about hunting, like getting attacked by a wild hog (I'll tell you that one later).

I did a good job on his air conditioner and gave him a fair price. We talked some more and I got to know more about him and the TV show. He's very intelligent and a good businessman. I felt honored to be able to spend some time with him. He also gave me some souvenirs and autographs from the other *Duck Dynasty* guys, which I shared with some friends.

The following year a different air conditioner broke down. So I went back out to Willie's and fixed it. When I got done, Willie said, "Mountain Man, come on over here. I want to talk to you."

I went around back to what I call his man cave, and he said, "Mountain Man, what are you doing next Thursday?"

I said, "Well, nothing, I don't reckon."

"How would you like to be in a film shoot?"

"Yeah, hey, that sounds good. I ain't doing nothing."

"Okay, fine," he said. "I'll call you Wednesday night and give you directions how to get out to my daddy's house."

When I arrived, I walked down an old dirt road to an open field. There were trucks, people, and camera equipment everywhere. I thought the film shoot was a little commercial or something. I didn't know what was going on.

I walked up to Willie and said, "Willie, what is this?"

He said, "This is A&E, Mountain Man. This is nation-wide television."

They were shooting a scene. He invited me out a little early to meet different folk and see what they were doing. Everyone I talked to was just amazed at the way I talked. They wanted my voice on their cell phone's voicemail message: "Hey, this is Jim, I'm not available now. Call me back in a little while."

They'd play it back and say, "Boy, that's it, Mountain Man! I appreciate that." And they took off running across the field to do their work. They really did like me. It was a privilege to be there.

They didn't get around to filming my part that day, so I just observed all that was taking place.

The next day was my part: the scene where I bought the squirrel. They were very pleased with how everything turned out and decided to call me back for another scene, and then another show, and another, and another.

I was in Willie's office one day after my popularity grew on the show. He said, "Mountain Man, when you were running them hills up in Tennessee as a kid, did you ever think you'd be on TV on a show like this?"

I said, "Not in a million years, Willie." And then I said, "What do you think, Willie? Did you ever think you would go into something like this?"

"Not in a million years, Mountain Man. Yes, God has been good to us, ain't he?"

"Yep. He works in mysterious ways."

Meeting Jase and Getting Baptized

While filming the *Duck Dynasty* series, I got to know Jase. We'd meet up in the duck call room and Jase would have his Bible around or if he didn't, he'd go get it and we'd have a Sunday school class in the duck call room. I remember thinking,

This guy is really sincere. He is really, truly with the Lord. A godly man.

I really enjoyed my conversations with Jase. My dog Buddy would come along and just lie on the floor and fall asleep in the cedar shavings. Then Buddy would suddenly sneeze. Jase would look at Buddy and sneeze too. I guess they both didn't like the cedar chips.

Some of the other Duck Commander guys would be in the room with us like Godwin and Martin, but they just let Jase and me talk. I was thinking I was a pretty good old boy. I was brought up right. Mama and Daddy took us to church, Sunday school, prayer meetings, and devotional studies. I was baptized a few times. Daddy was a deacon in church and a Sunday school teacher. Both parents were always helping with missions, trying to encourage donations and get missions started. We always had prayer at the table and Daddy was the one to say the blessing.

But you know, good works or good things parents or churches do for us don't earn us God's gift of salvation. Jase began to point out things in my life that didn't need to be there and challenged me to deal with what the Bible calls the old man or the old self. He started going after me like he was hunting a deer. I didn't always like what he told me, but I knew he was right.

In junior high I put my faith on the back burner and didn't keep God first in my life. I did a lot of things I'm not proud of over the years. It's easy to fall away, but God has given each of us a conscience so that we know when we're doing wrong. If you don't feel bad after doing something wrong, then maybe you've drifted away too far. I think it was the Lord convicting me and protecting me for what he had for me in the future. God doesn't give up on us. He's got plans for you whether you know it or not. I believe the Lord had plans for me, and I wanted to be a better man through Jesus Christ our Lord.

The great thing about knowing Jesus is that we can mess up and ask for forgiveness, and the Bible says the good Lord will forgive us. But my desire grew to deal with my old way of living, and Jase wanted to "give this boy a dunk in the water." He gave me a lot of Bible verses to take home to read.

As time went on, I got to know all the Robertsons. Each of them is as good as gold. I ate at their house a few times and went hunting with them. I also went to their church. Alan, Phil's oldest son, was the preacher back then. I really enjoyed it and started going all the time.

During the film shoot where I was on the conveyer belt in the canoe, I felt strongly that I wanted to repent and turn away from my old life, fully commit my life to Jesus Christ, and get re-baptized. I went outside to get a breath of fresh air and knelt down next to the muddy tires on Phil's four-wheel drive truck.

I had been hunting with the Robertsons a week or two before and Phil and I had talked about how Jase and I had been meeting in the duck call room to talk about the Bible. We also talked about my need to get right with the Lord. Phil knelt down next to me.

I said, "Mr. Phil, I think I'm ready to be baptized."

Phil stood up and a big smile came to his face. He opened the door to where they were filming and hollered, "Hey, Jase! Mountain Man is ready! Mountain Man is ready!"

We finished up the scene and I said, "Well, I need to go get some clothes to change into and I'll be up at the church."

And they said, "Hurry up, Mountain Man!"

I drove home—it's only about four miles away—and grabbed some clothes. I contacted my brother on the way, and he and his wife went to the church. When I got there, the whole Robertson family was there—every one of them.

I remember going under that water and seeing flashes of light. I thought it might be the light of the Holy Spirit, but it was Willie taking pictures when I was in the water. I came up out of the water feeling good—a new man. There was that light again, Willie snapping pictures. So I guess now if I ever mess up, Willie can show me the pictures and say, "Mountain Man, do you remember this?"

I'm not sure if he'd do that, but he's not going to have to. Since returning to a growing faith in Jesus Christ and affirming that faith through baptism, I continue to keep the Lord first in my life and serve him.

Being on the show is a God-send. But even better than being famous is knowing Jesus Christ. I'm committed to be a godly man and follow God each day. I want to use the platform God's provided to speak out and reach out, turning others toward the kingdom of God.

Psalm 139:14 says,

> *I will praise You, for I am fearfully and*
>   *wonderfully made;*
> *Marvelous are Your works,*
> *And that my soul knows very well.*

In order to keep a slow profile, you have to be at peace with yourself and the way God has made you. People have always given me a hard time for the way I talk. But I've come to see that it's been a blessing to be different. Phil once told me, "You've got them all fooled. You think quicker than you talk. And that's a good thing."

How do you feel about yourself? It's okay to be different. Think about what makes you unique and see it as a benefit not a curse. You are marvelous and Jesus loves you just the way you are.

PART TWO

KEEPIN' A SLOW PROFILE

2

Slowing Down Makes You Stronger

The weather was dry the opening day of squirrel season. Every step was like walking on Corn Flakes. All the crunching was making me hungry for cereal, so I knew I had to catch me a squirrel for supper.

I'm busted now, I thought. *They've heard me. I've got to get quieter.* So I sat down on a log for thirty minutes and looked for a quieter way to walk. I waited for a bunch of crows to call and then made my move. They created enough noise to drown out my steps. A woodpecker sounded off and I had another chance to make a move. I finally reached some leaves that were moist and was able to continue to move through the woods without scaring off the squirrels.

I made my way through the woods a little at a time, stopping periodically to listen. I could hear little nuts dropping. Emm-hmmm. There was something gnawing on the hickory nut tree. I moved slowly and kept still so the squirrel wouldn't see my movement and run away. The squirrel finished eating one nut and shook the branch. He then reached for another nut. I eased my gun up real slow, put the bead on him, and *pow*. One shot dropped the squirrel.

For squirrel hunting, walking hastily will get you nowhere. But slowing down, keeping quiet, and moving cautiously will mean the difference between going hungry and having something to eat later that day. Every step you take in the woods is important. Under one of those leaves might be a dry twig. If it snaps and a squirrel hears it, all the quiet walking you've done will be a waste of time and you'll have to wait again for another squirrel to show up.

I think these truths also apply to everyday life. Sometimes the very best thing you can do is get still. Don't just slow down; you have to stop because you don't know the way to go. Waiting on the Lord will give you the answers.

I know we don't like to wait. Patience is a hard virtue to learn. That reminds me of two old men who would go fishing on Sportsman Club Lake in Portland, Tennessee. They would stay out there for hours, but when they came back to the bank in that old wooden boat, they always had some of the biggest catfish that I'd ever seen. I asked them, "How'd y'all catch them? What bait did you use?" They said, "Patience, my son. Patience. That's how we caught 'em." Someone who can sit out on a lake long enough to catch two or three really big catfish has patience. By having patience, they came back with enough catfish to feed them for two or three days, not just a little snack.

Find a Place to Be Still

The Bible says in Psalm 46:10, "Be still, and know that I am God." A great way to be still is to have a place where you can be still. Sometimes I just have to get out in the woods in a tree to be still. It's important to get off by yourself some- where. Then you don't have other things bothering you.

The Bible says in Romans 1:20 that God's invisible attri- butes are clearly seen and understood by everyone. One way to know that he is God is by looking at his creation—a hum- mingbird, a majestic mountain, a clear lake, or a flower in bloom. An old hawk might fly over and send you a message from God, helping you to be still.

I love to get out my favorite fishing lures, rod and reel and head out in my boat. Or maybe I take my gun into the woods and sit in a deer stand. I might kill something or I might not. But I'm content and can be still and know that he is God.

Find a spot where you can be still. Try going outside into God's creation. All of it was created for us to look at and enjoy. It'll put you in a different mind-set of peace and stillness.

Practice Peace and Stillness

Why don't people have patience? Because they haven't slo- wed down enough to find it. It doesn't come all at one time. Just try to slow down for ten minutes and see what happens.

Practicing peace and stillness means you don't act hastily in a situation, leaving no time to think. Move cautiously and ask God to give you the answer. Sometimes it might take a while to get that answer. It's not like rubbing a genie bottle. Sometimes you have to come to a complete stop and wait. I like to stop my thoughts completely and just listen. You're living too fast if you have no time to reflect. It's hard to see God's signs if you're going a mile a minute.

If you've already acted and gone too far, you might have to go into reverse, back up, and change your trail. Changing your trail is what the Bible calls *repentance*. Turning from your own way and going God's way brings peace because true peace comes from knowing Jesus Christ and trusting him each day. When you settle things with the Lord, then you're at peace with God and can be at peace with yourself.

There are many benefits of maintaining your peace through patience and stillness. You're more relaxed and less uptight. It's healthier. People tend to get along with you better. People will come to you for advice if you have patience. I find bringing peace to someone very fulfilling. Best of all, when we are still, it's easier to hear what God has to say because our minds are clear.

The Lord talks to me and he'll talk to you too. He doesn't usually use words like, "Hey Tim, this is what you need to do." He puts thoughts into my head. But I have to be aware of those thoughts, which then helps me to make the right decisions.

Thinking Slow Can Save a Life

Keepin' a slow profile doesn't mean you always move slowly or that you take your good ol' time unnecessarily when you really need to take action. It's about being purposeful with your life so you do the right thing.

There was a time I was doing air-conditioning work in Nashville. I was working with another guy and he was putting up a sheet of metal between two joists in the basement. All of a sudden I heard a bunch of yelling and water spilling everywhere. He had busted a water pipe and in the excitement dropped a three-by-four piece of metal on his arm. The sharp corner slit open the inside of his forearm a good four inches long, two and a half inches wide, and a good inch deep. It hit the artery and you could see the muscle.

This was one time I had to get in a bit of a hurry, but I didn't panic. I came down the steps as fast as I could. First I looked at his face and it was white as a sheet. I knew he was going into shock and said, "Let me see it." He lifted his hand off the cut and I saw the severity of what had happened. Blood started to shoot out of the wound a good seven feet across the room in rhythm with his heartbeat. Some of the blood hit me and I said, "Put your hand back on." I knew I had to apply a tourniquet.

I saw an old cane fishing pole and broke off a chunk of it. I ran to the truck and found an extra shirt, ripped off the sleeve, wrapped it around the wound, tied a knot, took the piece of cane and made the tourniquet. I slowed down and talked real easy to him, "You're going to be all right." I called

911 and loosened up the tourniquet periodically to let the blood circulate while we waited for the ambulance.

I was really concerned about his arm since the metal had cut through his nerves. He did get some damage from the cut, but he was happy to be alive.

The EMT who came to the house asked me, "Did you put the tourniquet on?"

"Yeah. Did I mess him up?"

"No. You saved his life. He would have bled to death."

I was moving fast, but I was thinking slow. I reckon I saved a man's life by not getting all excited. That's just my nature to be calm. I give all the credit to the Lord. I believe he put the thoughts into my head—what to look for and what to do.

Of course we nicknamed him Scar after that. He didn't mind too much. I'm sure he was glad to be alive to talk about it.

Some people say, "Ol' Mountain Man doesn't get too excited over anything." Thankfully in this situation I stayed calm. But it's also important to slow down and think about your everyday decisions. Let God guide your thoughts and then act. This is a sure way to keep your life on track with the Lord.

Slow Down to Care

While sitting at a red light on the way to the airport, I saw a guy holding an old cardboard sign. I couldn't read it. He wanted something. I looked at that fella and wanted to help, but I didn't have much cash. Just a five, ten and a one. I usually don't carry much cash. I then realized he wanted a ride, but I was headed in another direction to catch a plane. I fumbled through my billfold and was going to give him the five, but yelled out, "Hey!" and held out the $10 bill.

His eyes went from nearly asleep to the most beautiful, big eyes I've ever seen. People behind me were honking. He took the money and said, "God bless you, brother."

With the busy traffic around me and while rushing to the airport, I'm so glad I was at peace within so that I could stop and care, even if it was for only a few moments.

Slow Down to Listen to Others

I was in a hurry the other day to get to the radio station for my show. I passed an old guy in overalls who said, "Hey, Mountain Man. How you doin'?"

I said, "Hey, good to see you. Take care."

He said, "Where are you goin' in such a hurry?"

I said, "I gotta go to the radio station."

"Well, I just want to shake your hand and tell you I'm proud of you for what you're doing on the show."

His comments slowed me down in my tracks. Even Mountain Man was in a hurry. I believe God sent this old guy in overalls to remind me to slow down and listen to what others have to say. I was encouraged and would have missed out if I hadn't stopped to have a conversation with this man God put in my path.

These words from Isaiah 40:29–31 encourage me:

[God] gives power to the weak,
And to those who have no might He increases
* strength.*
Even the youths shall faint and be weary,
And the young men shall utterly fall,
But those who wait on the Lord
Shall renew their strength;
They shall mount up with wings like eagles,
They shall run and not be weary,
They shall walk and not faint.

If you're feeling weak or weary, God has power for you. He will renew your strength as you slow down, are still, and find peace in Jesus Christ. Try turning off your cell phone or the TV for a few hours and get outside. Go find yourself a quiet place and just listen. You'll catch your squirrel, and more importantly, I believe you'll find the strength you need to walk the trail God has for you.

3

Keep First Things First

When I first started working at Popeyes, everything was running wild. I was fixing all the equipment for eight different restaurants, which was torment for a while. I was trying to do it all myself instead of giving it to the Lord. I'd get upset and say, "Look, I can't do it all at one time. Just have faith that I'll get 'r done."

After everyone got to know me and the good work that I did, they had faith in me. As things went more smoothly, I caught myself thinking, *I sure am good at fixing this stuff. Everybody likes me. Hey, I'm the man.* But then one night I thought, *Wait a minute. Where is this success coming from? I'm taking too much credit for myself.* Keeping God first means we realize who's doing what.

So I said a prayer, "Thank you, Lord, that I have a good job. It's just what I want." The good Lord knew I needed a good job because I had a little baby to raise. But God also wanted me to put him first and keep him first.

Keep Your Faith Up Front

I can't think of a better way to keep God first than starting out the day with prayer. The first thing many people do in the morning is brush their teeth. Prayer is even more important than that. Prayer is like turning the key to start your car or truck. It's the first step to get you rolling. Without faith first, I feel like it's not going to be as good of a day.

It's not always easy to pray. But be sure to start and end your day with prayer, and try to get in a few in-betweeners here and there too. Proverbs 3:6 says that when we acknowledge the Lord, he will direct our steps. I don't want to get lost in life. I've gotten lost in the woods far too many times. I want the Lord to direct my steps. So I choose to acknowledge him all day long in my thoughts and prayers.

Someone who puts faith first is happy to be alive another day. I try to enjoy everything I can. I avoid getting upset, correcting others, or letting others' actions ruin my day. I just focus on God and being who I am. Without faith I couldn't do it.

The horse doesn't belong before the cart. It's important to keep God up front. I don't want to look like I'm lazy because I'm not. I'm slower than many people, but God made me this way. He gives me time to think things out and not just react. This helps me keep my faith in front of worry. Slowing down gives you the chance to see how God brings things together. Your timing might be slower, but you'll end up doing the right thing.

Faith helps you live through each day, and to be prepared if today is your last day. Without faith first, you're going to end up running in circles like a beagle hound chasing a rabbit. People who do more things and have more stuff often have more problems and are unhappy. Those who put faith first still have problems, but will have more smiles.

Avoid Distractions

Distractions can get in the way of hitting your target. Even good things can get in the way of the best God has for us. Work is good, but if it gets in the way of family, it's a distraction. Talking is good, but if it gets in the way of listening, it's a distraction.

I love PayDay candy bars. But they have been both helpful and distracting more than once. One time I was out hunting and was getting really hungry about 10:30 a.m. I pulled out a PayDay candy bar. A deer happened to come out at the same time and the noise scared it away. I've learned to eat the PayDay before daylight. Deer just think it's a squirrel rattling something.

Another time I went out to go hunting and the woods were full of hunters. I had scouted out that same spot the day before and no one was around. But the next day it seemed like every other tree had a person in it. Jonathan was with me so we searched for two spots. I found him one but had to walk a good distance farther and struggle through a mass of briars before finally crawling up into my own tree.

I was hungry and pulled out my PayDay and stuffed half of the bar into my mouth with the wrapper still on the other side. Just then a deer came into the clearing and started walking toward me. I watched as the wrapper slid off the end of the candy bar and slowly spiraled to the ground like a helicopter propeller. I thought for sure the deer would get spooked and run. Instead it watched the wrapper and I shot the deer. It was a payday on that deer and I have a PayDay to thank. So I guess something good can either be good or bad depending on what's most important. Either turn that distraction into something that works good in your life or get rid of it.

Many distractions keep us from the best God has. Looking for the right partner can be good, but if she's getting between you and God Almighty, you may need to walk away. Spouses need to be godly. Being unequally yoked is a big headache and a distraction.

I don't need to describe all the distractions that can come your way. You know what's distracting you. If it's keeping you from what's really important in your life, it's time to deal with that distraction and refocus.

Family Time Is Valuable Time

It seems these days that everyone's on the run. Mom and Dad have to work. Kids are involved in many activities. I've seen that the best way to keep a family tight is at the dinner table.

Every chance you get, sit down for a meal, say the blessing, and eat together as a family—especially if everyone is home. As you're eating, talk about what happened that day, your friends, livestock (that's for you country folk), or anything on your mind.

Don't try to chomp your food down too fast unless you're starving to death and are afraid someone will take the last chicken leg. Don't grab your food and go sit by the TV or run up to your room, lie on the bed, and start texting.

Dinnertime is a time out, so slow down. Turn off the TV. Look at everyone eyeball-to-eyeball and communicate. You might not get that time very often and you'll be glad for that time later in life.

Eating together was important to my family growing up. We kids were always pretty hungry and wanted to make sure we had a good seat at the dinner table. Daddy, Mama, and the three of us kids would talk to each other. It was probably a little easier back then since the only thing we had to run off to was a TV show. We only got three channels so there really wasn't much to watch and Daddy didn't let us go off somewhere with our food. He said, "Boy, you're going to spill that drink on the carpet. Come in here and eat at the table and let's talk."

And that's what we did. The dog was by our side. We made sure Rep or Nubs got a scrap. My parents asked us about school, grades, and what we'd been doing. It was important at our dinner table to stay in tune with each other. The dinner table is where things can come out and where you can sort out things.

My dad showed me a lot of love and taught me how to love. Ironically my dad and mom didn't often tell me they loved me. People say you need to hear "I love you," but we knew it as kids and we showed it as a family. I know people who say, "I love you," but they don't show it and you can't see it. The only way to know they love you is with their words not their actions. I'd rather have the actions that show love than only words with good intentions.

Some of the ways my dad showed me love was by taking me fishing and spending time with me. If you're a parent, help your kid find a hobby that you can do with them. My dad also took time to talk to me if I had a problem. So did my mom. That really helped me get through some hard times.

Sometimes we would watch TV as a family. We had to get up and turn the channel because there was no remote control. Being the youngest, I was the remote control. Far too often I heard, "Hey, go turn to channel 4...now turn to channel 5."

We had our first black-and-white TV in Hallock, Minnesota, and every now and again the picture would go fuzzy. Daddy had a special technique to fix the problem. He'd stomp his foot on the floor and the vibrations would make the TV come back on. When color TV came out, you couldn't get Daddy out of the recliner during the ballgames. But he still took time to take me out hunting and fishing and taught me how to clean all the game.

When Jonathan was younger I used to read books to him. It usually took me three months to finish one book. He loved the book *The Dog with Golden Eyes*. First it was really interesting to him. He listened for a chapter and then fell asleep. Then he fell asleep after just three-quarters of a chapter. Then one-half a chapter. Then two pages. Then a page. Then I only read one sentence and he was out. He told me, "Daddy, you just put me to sleep the way you talk." Maybe I should go into sleep therapy or read children's books so they go to sleep at the end of a long day when their parents are tired out.

I've heard it said that family members can get the worst of us. Keep family at the top of your priorities and do what you can to give them your best.

Never Give Up on Your Kids

I continued the tradition of eating as a family with my son. His mama would cook. We knew it was ready because the smoke alarm would go off.

I'd say, "Hey, the smoke alarm went off. It's time to eat."

"It'll taste burnt, Daddy."

"Just break off a piece. It might be a bit raw in the middle, but there's part of it in there that'll be good to eat."

I'm just having fun. It wasn't that bad.

It was wise to put at least half of what you were going to eat on your plate before Jonathan started. That boy loved to eat and he ate fast. We had good communication at the table back then.

Sadly my wife and I got divorced when Jonathan was about seven years old. Jonathan spent most of his time with me, my mama and daddy. When I was at work, Mama and Daddy took care of him. I'd go over to the house to get him and he didn't want to come home. That hurt my feelings. But I don't blame Jonathan. His parents were divorced and he was an only child.

When my son reached adolescence, things got harder. I couldn't keep up with who he was hanging out with and it was a bad situation. It's easy to pick up bad ways from others, which leads to worse things. There was a time when he got pretty down on himself and it was really hard to communicate with him and help him. Sitting down at the table ended. He was always out with his friends.

I was trying to keep up with it, but I lost that discipline and communication with my son for a while. Proverbs 13:24 says that those who love their children discipline them promptly. Proverbs 3:12 says that the Lord disciplines those he loves. We need to follow that example as we make loving our children a priority.

Thankfully all through the arguing we always had love for each other. Jonathan has always liked a good laugh and laughter is a good sign. When they quit laughing, you know something is wrong. And for a while, he didn't want to laugh.

I never gave up. Some people say you need to hit rock bottom sometimes. But I never wanted to see Jonathan hit rock bottom. I knew I had to keep trying and praying. I had a lot of people praying for him. I'm thankful for Jeff and Laura who prayed earnestly with me for my son.

Jonathan became a great swimmer and was a captain of the swim team in high school. He started watching what he ate. He lifted weights and kept his body toned. Now he's into health foods. He quit messing around with the wrong kind of people and found some godly women to date. Through prayer and never giving up Jonathan made a complete turnaround.

He loves me and tells me he loves me all the time. Of course I tell him I love him too. We show love for each other. I'm so proud of my son. He's been able to come to some events with me, which has been very rewarding for both of us. I'm proud of the turnaround he made in his life and that he turned to the Lord. Perseverance paid off.

Go to Church

My daddy always took us to church and we were together every Sunday. If I said I wasn't going to go, he'd get out the belt. Once I got there I enjoyed it.

Some prefer to do their yard work on Sunday instead of rest or go to church. Hey, I let the grass grow a lot of times. I'm not going to be out there mowing grass instead of going to church. If I can go to church, I'm going to go.

Maybe you haven't gone to church and you've always heard, "Well, so and so is a hypocrite, and if that's what it means to be a Christian, I don't want that." Don't let someone else's hypocrisy be an excuse not to go to church. And don't ever let it give you an excuse not to turn to the Lord. There are always bumps on the road of life. But when God is first in our lives, he'll be with us and can turn things around on a dime. Following God and putting first things first will always pay off in the long run.

It's hard to keep first things first. We all lose our way sometimes. Matthew 6:33–34 records these words of Jesus:

> *But seek first the kingdom of God and His righteousness, and all these things shall be added to you. Therefore do not worry about tomorrow.*

Are you too busy with everyday life? Don't neglect to put God's kingdom first. Slow down. Take time to pray and go to church. Say "I love you" to those you love and prove it with your actions. Make sure your family gets your attention, and try to eat meals with your family regularly.

If you will keep first things first, you don't have to worry and can trust God to take care of your needs.

4

Humor Tickles like a Feather

When I lived in Tennessee, there was a boy in my class we called Squarehead. You want to know how he got his name? One day in Sunday school class my brother and some of his friends took out a ruler and measured each side of this boy's head. It was perfectly square.

My class was next door and I remember hearing *bam, bam, bam* coming from my brother's classroom. I asked Bill, "What were y'all doing in there?"

Bill said, "Oh, that was just ol' Squarehead banging his head up against the wall. I think he's trying to stay awake." Maybe that's how his head got square.

Back when haircuts were a dollar, we joked that it cost Squarehead four dollars to get a haircut—a dollar for each side. Squarehead was a great kid, but he fell for a few of our pranks.

One time a few of us went fishing and camped out overnight. As soon as Squarehead fell asleep, we tied his fishing line around half a concrete block. We took the pole and slung the block out into the lake. *Plunk*. Then we reeled the line in a bit so that his pole was bent.

I could hardly sleep.

When Squarehead got up and saw his pole bent over, he ran to see what he'd caught.

I said, "Man, you got a good one."

Squarehead pulled on the line and said, "It's a giant turtle!"

Another guy told him, "You've got a log."

But Squarehead insisted, "No I can feel it! It's pulling!" We all just let him believe he had a big one on his line.

He pulled his catch right up to the edge of the bank and the line broke. Squarehead threw his pole down in anger. He again said, "It was a giant turtle and I know it!"

That was the greatest fight with a concrete block I ever saw.

A week later in school we all told Squarehead about our joke.

"Nope, it was a turtle. I felt it pulling." For a good month we tried to get him to believe the truth. He insisted it was a turtle.

That was just one of the many pranks I was a part of growing up.

The Class Clown

I've always loved to make people laugh. Sometimes I got in trouble at school because I was making the class laugh too much. They laughed at my voice and my off-the-wall comments. I had a real deep cough that sounded like the loudest honk you ever heard. It would echo to the other side of the cafeteria. *Ka-bonk!* I could even say words while I was coughing.

On the mischievous side, one time I stuck a nail in the crevice between my chair's seat and leg and twanged the nail while the teacher was speaking. *Boing, boing, boing, boing.* The teacher stopped. I stopped. She started talking and I started again with the nail. *Boing, boing, boing, boing.* I did that for a few days, but then got caught and paddled real hard so I stopped for good.

Sometimes I'd put my boots on the opposite feet and walk down the hall. I adjusted my pant legs so that everyone was sure to notice.

I also drew pictures of funny-looking animals with human heads, which I'd pass around the room. I just liked to make people laugh.

Pranks

I've done a few things you should never try at home. Two buddies and I climbed a water tower one night. There were lots of pigeons up there and we scared them off so we could have some fun with their eggs. When some employees got off their shift at 11 p.m., we tossed the eggs over the edge onto the walkway and on top of their cars. We overheard them discussing where the eggs were coming from. They speculated that other employees were playing pranks on them, and we were up there laughing. The water tower was so high they couldn't hear us.

Besides the fishing trick we played on Squarehead, we also found a little ol' garter snake and put it inside the desk where he did his homework. The drawers shut up real tight, so we knew it wouldn't escape in the house.

Shortly after supper I was sitting outside shooting flies with my BB gun when I saw Squarehead's mama coming toward me. She had a mean look on her face, and buddy, when she got to me, she told me about the snake.

If she'd had that snake in her hand, or a stick, she'd a whooped me good with it. She said, "Don't you ever put a snake in a drawer again."

I said, "I won't."

She said, "If you forget, I'll spank you myself." She was the one who found the snake in the desk and it scared her to death.

Even when we didn't pull a prank on Squarehead, he made us laugh in other ways. One time he was playing basketball and the ball bounced off the court and rolled in some cat poop. We warned him, but he insisted it was just mud.

We said, "Squarehead, you need to go wash your hands." He didn't listen, but my brother and I noticed that he kept bringing his hand to his nose to smell his fingers. It took him several whiffs to convince him we were right. Finally he said he had to go home.

Pranks and the funny things that happened growing up showed me how good laughter can be.

Humor Is Good for the Soul

I think I inherited my enjoyment of laughter from my dad. He has a good sense of humor and can find the positive in any situation. Daddy's always been a godly man and brightens the day through humor. If things get heated, he can just make a joke out of it and turn it right into laughter. That's what they liked about him at work.

Whenever he'd run into a situation that might get someone bent out of shape, he said, "There's worse things in the world than that." I guess being a World War II veteran gave him perspective on life. The plane he was on was shot down and they barely made it across enemy lines before ditching the plane. It's good to remember that it can always be worse. You could have just got bit by a fox with a foaming mouth, you know.

Daddy also talked a lot about a guy he worked with at the plant in Portland, Tennessee. Ray never got upset. No matter how down everyone was, Ray came in and had a way of poking fun to put a smile on anyone's face at any given point in time. He could make a dog smile. Ray never took anything too serious except his Bible and God. I remember my daddy telling me, "Even as mad as I get sometimes at workers who come in late all beat up because they were up all night doing something they weren't supposed to, Ray always manages to bring a smile to someone's face at the drop of a hat."

Laughter is good for the soul. It just makes you feel better. I find no greater fulfillment than to get someone smiling when they're discouraged. When people are really down and out, try and see if you can get a laugh out of them. Better yet, get them busting-out laughing. Even if it lasts for just a moment or two, it's a relief to change their mood. I take joy when I get them laughing. If someone is still sour, tell them, "Hey, you don't want your face to freeze like that. Try a smile."

Humor Releases Stress

Laughter is one way I like to relieve stress. If my comments, jokes, or laughter doesn't lighten the mood of a tense situation, I just pull out a feather from my back pocket and tickle them under the chin. I use humor like a pressure-release valve.

When I worked at Popeyes, I worked with a guy named Joe. I was the service technician and Joe supervised all the restaurant managers. I made more money than he did. He couldn't figure that one out.

One day Joe gave me a call about a fryer that had been broken for a while. He's the kind of guy that when he wants something done, he wants it done yesterday. I'd been real busy over in Vicksburg working my tail off when he called.

He told me I needed to get the fryer fixed. I told him I was working on refrigeration at another store. He was laying on the pressure and I raised my voice back at him, "Look, my job is not as easy as you think. What have *you* been doing today?"

"What do you mean, what have *I* been doing?"

Louisiana's summers are already hot and our argument just made things hotter.

The next thing I said was, "Well, Joe, I tell you what. If I could reach through this phone right now, I'd grab you by the hair and pull you through and work you over."

He said, "Well, if I could reach through this phone, I'd grab you and pull you through this line and we'd be gettin' at it."

Then all of a sudden I said, "Joe, I don't think we can reach through the phone and grab each other."

He said, "Naw, I guess we can't."

"What are we so mad about, anyway?"

"Nothing," he said.

"Well, I'll be over there in a little while and fix the fryer and we'll get 'r going."

"That sounds good," he said.

"Besides, we'd probably have got shocked trying to reach through these phones to grab each other," I said. And we turned a tense conversation into laughter. I guess we were both under so much pressure that we would have hurt each other if we were talking in person.

I just can't stand to argue. I've been around people that just want to argue. Sometimes it takes a little longer to get them out of their mood, but soon we're both laughing and in a happier atmosphere.

Laugh at Yourself

To break the ice when I'm on the road at events, all I have to do is open my mouth up and say, "Hey, y'all. I hope you brought some camping tents 'cause this speech might take a little while." That always gets them. Or "If y'all get bored, I think there's some coffee back yonder at the concession stand to keep you awake." Or "They'll probably drag me out of here before I get done with half this speech." Poking fun at myself is a great way to lighten the mood and let people know I want to have some fun.

Growing up, my brother Bill and I liked to fish together. We were out in the boat one day and I hung my lure in a tree by accident and wanted to get it free. Bill kept saying, "We'll go over there in a minute. Just another cast or two." I got tired of waiting and finally reached over and grabbed the paddle.

Bill also grabbed the paddle and we started a tug-of-war with the paddle, back and forth in the boat. And boy, I gave it the hardest yank that I could, pulling the paddle out of Bill's grip. I flew out of the boat into the water.

I was all wet and didn't know what to think. I handed him the paddle and crawled back in the boat. I didn't get too mad at Bill and we just went back to fishing. I did mess up the fishing spot though with my big splash. I was just happy because I won the tug-of-war. He's bigger than me, and I was glad to be stronger that day.

I like Psalm 16:11, which says,

You will show me the path of life;
In Your presence is fullness of joy;
At Your right hand are pleasures forevermore.

The next time you're tempted to get bent out of shape about something, try to laugh at yourself, find humor in the situation, or make the day a little brighter for someone else. If you stay on God's path, that means you'll be in his presence throughout the day and will experience joy.

I like to say that if humor doesn't work, use a feather—or whatever trick you have to make the world a little brighter. Add some "humor helper" to someone's day to make them happier.

If you have the energy to complain, use it to find something good. Count your blessings and help others count their blessings too. When things are hard, remember the words of Nehemiah 8:10:

> *"Do not sorrow, for the joy of the Lord is your strength."*

When's the last time you really laughed? Sometimes you need to slow down in order to see God's blessings and the funny parts of life. Remember to laugh at yourself and take the time to smile at those you pass on the street. Your attitude is sure to brighten someone else's day. And you'll find that God's joy will be your strength.

5

Look for Signs

I like the scene in the movie *Bruce Almighty* when Bruce is in his car crying out to God for guidance. Right after he asks God to give him a signal, he sees a traffic sign flashing, "CAUTION AHEAD." Bruce cries out again, "Give me a sign!" Just then a large truck pulls in front of him filled with signs that say, "Wrong Way," "Do Not Enter," "Stop," and "Dead End." He doesn't pay attention, gets upset at the driver, and recklessly passes him. Bruce runs into a light pole a short time later. He just didn't see the signs God was sending him.

I see signs from God all around me. My favorite sign on the road is "Slow Down." I see other signs, too, which I'll share with you in this chapter. God is always speaking. We just need to see what he's saying to us.

God Answers Prayers

When I got married, the doctor told us we could never have children. Something was missing from my wife's baby-maker machine. I prayed for a baby and she conceived the same night that I prayed. That baby's name is Jonathan. It was a sign to me that God answers prayers and that I was supposed to have a son. This miraculous sign gave me faith to believe everything would turn out for good, especially when things got really hard with Jonathan during his adolescent years.

Signs in God's Creation

An old guy who had lots of dogs used to take me hunting. After he died, I didn't go hunting for a long time. It just wasn't the same without him. When I finally went out to hunt, I went to an old spot he showed me. I wasn't in a hurry that day. I got up in the old tree and waited. He used to tell me, "Wait and the deer will come down that hill." I had him on my mind as I was out there.

Sure enough, along came a four-point buck. I shot. It was a good hit and I heard the deer fall. The clouds had been covering the sky all morning. I looked up to pray and said, "Thank you, Lord, for this bounty. Thank you for allowing me the time with Adolphus while he was here on this earth."

All of a sudden the skies broke in one little area and the sun peeked through to light up my tree. The sun shone no other place except the tree I was in. The clouds closed the gap a few minutes later. It was a sign from heaven for me because I had listened to an old friend and thanked the Lord for his provision. Some might call that light an amazing coincidence. Or maybe they wouldn't have noticed it at all. For me it was a sign of God's blessing.

Signs from God

Without signs, we'd just be running in circles not knowing which way to go. It's important to know what those signs mean. Signs can lead us into righteous paths in the Lord and show us what he would have us to do.

Every day you wake up you see the world around you. Have you ever seen God's creation as one big sign to you? The Bible says that in the beginning God created the heavens and the earth. Every time you see a tree, it should tell you, "God made that tree." Man can take credit for planting trees, but where did trees come from? Trees and the rest of God's creation were put here on earth for us. Psalm 19:1–4 shows that creation can speak to us about God.

The heavens declare the glory of God;
And the firmament shows His handiwork.
Day unto day utters speech,
And night unto night reveals knowledge.
There is no speech nor language
Where their voice is not heard.
Their line has gone out through all the earth,
And their words to the end of the world.

Gideon's Signs

I like the story of Gideon in the Bible. One day an angel showed up and told Gideon God's plan to save his people. But Gideon had a hard time believing he was the right guy for the job. So God used multiple signs to encourage him.

The phrase, "I'm going to lay out a fleece and see what happens," comes from the story of Gideon in Judges 6. Gideon's fleece was a literal fleece—the woolly covering of a sheep or goat. Gideon took a fleece and set it outside on the ground overnight. If the dew was only on the fleece and not the ground, that would be a sign from God. That's what happpened. You'd think that would be enough. But God gave Gideon another sign. Gideon set out a fleece again the next night. The following morning the ground around the fleece was wet with dew, but the fleece was dry. Gideon knew that God had chosen him to be the leader to help save his people.

God used signs all throughout the Bible to speak to people, and I believe he still uses supernatural signs today. I don't think we should *seek* signs. Jesus reprimanded those who demanded signs and only followed him because of the miracles he did. But we can *look* for signs because they're one way we can see what God is doing and hear what he is saying to us.

Signs Can Direct Us to Help Others

There are signs when squirrels have been in an area. They leave cuttings on the ground where they've eaten. While you're hunting, you have to sit and listen for the little ol' nuts to fall. Or you listen for a branch making a noise. I always stare at the main trunks of the tree line, looking for any movement. My eyes are really good at catching movement. It's something I think you develop. You can also develop sensitivity to seeing signs with people.

When I first meet a person, I immediately look for signs that help me know what I'm getting myself into. A sign of a person in need could be a yard full of cigarette butts and whiskey bottles, or nasty words, anger, cursing, or maybe just a sad countenance. A smile, a Bible, or a positive attitude are other signs. Sometimes you can't tell what's going on in a person's life by just looking at external signs. But if you look a little deeper, you can know what's going on so you can encourage them.

In the chapter "Slowing Down Makes You Stronger," I shared some stories about what happened when I just slowed down and took the time to listen or see the need around me. In each of those situations, I saw a sign. It was like getting a nudge from God to take care of something he thinks is important. If we slow down and pay attention, we'll get to help a lot of people and be blessed at the same time.

Slow Down to Read the Signs

As I've entered into the entertainment business, I continue to seek to be a godly man. But now there's so much more stuff coming at me. Every day I try to listen to what God is saying to me. I look for signs—the right people, the right places, the right choices. Sometimes I look for signs and get confused. Which way do I go? That's when I have to slow down. I need to keep it slow.

We all mess up. When we sin, we can pray for forgiveness and get back on the right track. That's the time to stop, back up, and reread the signs. God puts out signs, but the devil also puts out signs. That's why we need to pray. If you're still confused, then pray some more.

Getting signs from God might sound spooky or super spiritual. It's not. It's just realizing that God's really big and wants to speak to you. So he'll use whatever is around to help you see his path.

Look for signs. Ask yourself, "Is this the right sign or the wrong sign?" Then make sure you read the signs right. Read slooooow.

Don't seek signs. Seek God, but look for the signs he sends to you. The biggest sign you need to pay attention to is the same sign an angel gave to some shepherds about two thousand years ago. Luke 2:12 says:

> And this will be the sign to you: You will find a Babe wrapped in swaddling cloths, lying in a manger."

Jesus Christ is the sign God has given to everyone to show his love for the world. John 3:16 is my favorite Bible verse. It says that God so loved the world that he gave his only Son. You don't want to miss this sign of God's love for you.

God wants to communicate with you in other ways too. What signs do you see from God? Slow down enough to see them, and if necessary, stop, back up, and reread the signs God is putting in your life.

6

Don't Fall Out of the Boat

I've fallen out of the boat a few too many times…even as an adult. My brother Bill and I were running up the river in a boat catching bass. We turned into a slough (inlet), and a little ways in found ourselves a shallow spot and got the boat stuck on a stump.

I moved toward the middle of the boat so there'd be less weight in the front and Bill trimmed up the motor some. He began to move the boat forward into deeper water and I decided to head back to my seat.

Just as I was turning on one leg, he gunned the motor and we ran smack into another stump. *Boom.* The boat stopped and there was no way to balance on just one leg. I popped right out of the boat and into the water. *Foomf.*

I went all the way under the water fully clothed, wearing my work boots and a hat. My hat stayed on, but my cell phone got all wet. I was fully soaked. I looked like a squirrel in the water trying to get a leg up on the side and into the boat.

I was kind of upset at him. I said, "What did you have to take off for?"

He said, "I thought you were on your way to your seat. We hit that stump and, boy, the boat sure did stop fast."

"Yeah, I sure did rocket out of the boat."

This story makes me think of the stumps we hit in life sometimes. We're off balance so when we hit something hard, we end up getting thrown out of the boat. Balance and stability are important in a boat, and also in life.

Stand in the Center

If you've never been in a boat before, remember to stay in the center. Both you and the boat will stay balanced. When you're walking in the boat, walk in the center as much as you can. Try to keep your weight equal on each side so you're not tipsy.

This is also how you walk with God. You need to stay in the middle of the path he has for you. Matthew 7:13–14 quotes Jesus who said,

> *"Enter by the narrow gate; for wide is the gate and broad is the way that leads to destruction, and there are many who go in by it. Because narrow is the gate and difficult is the way which leads to life, and there are few who find it."*

Find the narrow path. Stay in the center. The closer you are to the edge, the easier it is to get off that path and get lost.

Guide yourself down the center of the path that God wants you to walk. That narrow path will lead you to Jesus' narrow gate.

It's also not so smart to stand while the motor is running. When the boat is going fast, you have to stay planted. If it stops, you'll keep going at full speed. Be prepared for whatever comes. If you're planted, you can handle a sudden change of direction.

God wants us to take a strong stance—not just in a boat so we don't fall out, but in life. That's one thing I've really respected about the Robertsons. They plant their feet firmly, take a stand, and don't back down. Psalm 1:3 tells what happens to a person who stays on the right path:

He shall be like a tree
Planted by the rivers of water,
That brings forth its fruit in its season,
Whose leaf also shall not wither;
And whatever he does shall prosper.

The Robertsons have hit some stumps along the way, but they haven't fallen out of the boat because their feet are firmly planted on the Word of God. Staying planted and balanced in the Word will prepare you to stand against what the enemy sends against you. Ephesians 6:10–11 encourages us to "be strong in the Lord and in the power of His might. Put on the whole armor of God, that you may be able to stand against the wiles of the devil." God gives us the armor we need for our battles so we can stand. You don't always know what the enemy will look like, but being prepared helps you stay strong in the Lord.

Storms of life can come out of nowhere and start shaking your boat. These storms can seem overwhelming. Take out your shield of faith and cover up during the storm. It will pass over and you'll get through.

Negative People Sink the Boat

I've seen plenty of people who are in a boat going nowhere and they want you to join them for the ride down the river. They always seem to have problems; their talk is negative most of the time; they don't go to church and don't want to talk about God; and they want you to listen to all their problems—at work and at home.

When this happens to me, their gloom becomes gloomy for me. Before I know it, I'm right there with them in a sinking boat with a hole going nowhere because the motor is broken.

Watch for people who will sink your boat: those who are known to be rowdy, aren't in touch with the Lord, drink, litter, use profanity, ignore people who need help, have no respect for elders, holler at people out the window.... Hey, don't yell at some old lady because it might just be my mama.

God wants us to slow down and try to help others with their problems. But sometimes there's only so much you can do.

Leave a Clean Trail

I like to hunt on the wildlife reserves and appreciate people who leave a clean trail out in the woods. They pick up after themselves and deal with their garbage properly.

I'm always surprised when people throw their trash carelessly on the ground. I do my best to clean up the check-in area so that those who manage the game reserve appreciate us and work to keep the grounds open for us to enjoy. If I see trash out in the woods, I put it in my pouch and dispose of it later. No matter where you hunt, do your best to leave it cleaner than it was before you got there. It shows respect and you're more likely to be able to hunt there next year.

God wants us to leave a clean trail in life too. He wants us to deal with our problems and not just leave them around for others to deal with. Leaving a clean trail is not just about going to church. Many who don't go to church leave clean trails. They make good choices and are serving God the best they can. And some who do go to church are making a mess and living as hypocrites.

Some people think that leaving a clean trail or godly living is boring and not fun. Godly living is actually exciting and full of adventure. It keeps us from falling out of the boat and helps us stay on the right path with the Lord. Sacrifices we make are always replaced with blessings.

It's also good to hang out with people who are leaving clean trails. The Bible says that bad company corrupts good habits. Hanging around good people is a breath of fresh air right off the Gulf. They help you stay firm in the Lord. Positive things happen. You laugh around them. Little things don't bother you. You don't have to sort through so much foul language any more. They will have their struggles, but you get an inner-soul feeling that encourages you to be like them.

Living the way the Lord wants you to produces a natural high. You will have a sense of fulfillment, knowing the Lord is working through you as you combine efforts with others working for the Lord. Godly living is like having a smiling dog looking at you instead of a growling dog ready to bite you. Godliness keeps you from falling out of the boat, stable and walking on God's trail.

I've fallen out of the boat way too many times—not just on the water but also in life. Are you asking God to help you stay in the center of his trail for your life? Don't move so quickly you fall out of the boat. Slow down and deal with your garbage, and make the effort to keep a clean trail. Be sure to find friends who are doing the same thing.

I like these two verses, one from 1 Corinthians 16:13 and the next from 1 Corinthians 15:58.

Watch, stand fast in the faith, be brave, be strong.

Be steadfast, immovable, always abounding in the work of the Lord, knowing that your labor is not in vain in the Lord.

The way you choose to live really makes a difference, both now and in the future. Choose the narrow path. Leaving a clean trail is an exciting way to live. Use the armor God has given to you, stand firm in your faith, and be strong in the Lord.

7

Small Seeds Grow Big Trees

'**ve** always been inspired by the story of Johnny Apple-seed. Johnny was an American pioneer and nurseryman who planted apple trees throughout Pennsylvania, Ohio, and other states in the early 1800s.

As I travel around the United States, I think about Johnny. Even though he lived a good long life, he didn't get to see the full fruit of his labor. I won't ever again see most of the people I meet, and often I don't know what good comes out of my time in different places. But I have an opportunity to plant good seeds in their lives. That's what Christ wants me to do, and that's what he wants you to do too.

I don't have any idea if the seeds I plant will grow into vines that bear good fruit. Every once in a while someone calls to thank me and tell me how well things are going with the Lord. But even if the ground doesn't appear to be fertile,

I'm going to plant the seeds anyway. I think that's our part. We continue to plant seeds and trust that God will do his part.

Jesus told a story about a farmer who went out to sow his seeds. Some fell on the side of the road. The birds ate those. Some fell among the rocks, but since their roots couldn't go very deep, they didn't last long when the sun beat on them. Some fell in the thorns, and those thorns choked out the seeds. And then some fell on the good ground, and they turned into a good crop.

Jesus' disciples didn't understand his story, so he explained it. I think it helps us to know how to plant good seeds, which Jesus said represents sharing the word of the kingdom of God. Matthew 13:19–23 says:

> When anyone hears the word of the kingdom, and does not understand it, then the wicked one comes and snatches away what was sown in his heart. This is he who received seed by the wayside. But he who received the seed on stony places, this is he who hears the word and immediately receives it with joy; yet he has no root in himself, but endures only for a while. For when tribulation or persecution arises because of the word, immediately he stumbles. Now he who received seed among the thorns is he who hears the word, and the cares of this world and the deceitfulness of riches choke the word, and he becomes unfruitful. But he who received seed on the good

ground is he who hears the word and understands it, who indeed bears fruit and produces.

As we slow down and take time to plant seeds in other people's lives, it's good to know what kind of ground we're sowing into. Johnny Appleseed didn't just scatter seeds randomly. He planted nurseries and built fences around the trees to protect them from wandering livestock. We can be smart and plant our seeds in good soil—in the lives of people who will bear good fruit.

We can also help people to understand the Word so the devil doesn't steal the truth from their hearts. We can help them get through hard times so they don't stumble and turn away from the Lord. And we can help others not get caught up in things of this world that choke out their life. This is what planting seeds is all about.

I want to have a heart that's ready for God's good seed. I haven't always tried to live a godly life, but through other people planting seeds in my life—like my parents or the Robertson family—I'm bearing good fruit today.

Godly Character Is Important

Phil Robertson has planted seeds in my life through his humor, talent, and ability to share his testimony. I heard him say that when you share the Word with other people, don't tell them what church you're from or mention your religion.

You'll just lose half the people you're talking to. Just talk about being godly. Phil's an effective messenger on a mission to spread the gospel. He's planted seeds in my life by just being a godly man and challenging others to be godly too.

A great way to plant seeds in people's lives is to have that godly character. Here are a few qualities that I've found helpful.

Obedience. Following the Ten Commandments is a good start for obedience. Most of them tell you what not to do. Jesus summed up all of God's law into two commandments: love God completely and love others generously. When people see us happy and obeying these two commandments, there's no better seeds that can be sown.

Wisdom. The Bible says that God's ways are higher than our ways. Real wisdom comes from God. Get that wisdom through prayer and staying close to God. I've also found a lot of wisdom as I read the book of Proverbs in the Bible. A chapter a day will get you through the book in a month. As you receive wisdom from God, you can sow that wisdom into someone else's life.

Self-control. One time I was so mad that I acted hastily while driving. I was driving fast and lost control of my truck. I hit a telephone pole and nearly killed me, the person in the truck with me, and my dog in the back. I realized that I was wrong and I shouldn't have been so angry. Uncontrolled anger just leads to bad things. We should have died in the crash. The Lord shielded all of us for sure. So whether it's anger or a negative expression of another emotion, God wants us to plant the seed of self-control when we feel like just letting it all go.

Kindness and respect. I was always very respectful when I went into houses for business. Some houses had people boozing, kids screaming, and heavy smoking. I would just do the job, be as nice as I could, and get out. Other times someone wanted to have a conversation. So I stopped what I was doing just to talk to him. The fulfillment that we both got out of the conversation was priceless. Sometimes I got in trouble with my boss for taking too long, but it was worth it to plant seeds of kindness and see a smile.

Faithfulness and integrity. I respect all the Robertsons because they just don't budge. They stick to the Word and do what's right. They continue to get opportunities to spread the message and they don't back down. The fruit from their lives has affected me and millions of other people. God's always good. He takes our efforts and does the real work of making seeds grow and bear fruit.

In 1 Corinthians 3:5–6, the apostle Paul said that he was just a servant to help people believe. He planted the seeds, another person watered them, but it was God who "gave the increase." We all need to just do our part, and God will do his part by making those seeds grow.

Look for Opportunities

The least I can do for the Lord is plant seeds in other's lives. God sent his only Son down here to preach the gospel to us, and what happened to Jesus? He went through torment and died on the cross. Think of that happening to your only son. For a man to do that much for me, I think this is the least that I can do back. Sometimes I feel like I can't do enough back.

I talk slow and move slow, but I believe keeping a slow, steady pace helps me to see the opportunities God brings my way. It's not about me seeking out how many accomplishments *I* can make. God wants me to look for opportunities that *he* brings. I think the Lord smiles every time I do that.

Small seeds grow big trees. God wants us to be faithful with the small opportunities we have each day because he knows he can turn them into big fruit for his kingdom. Each opportunity is like a surprise. Maybe I've been riding around in my truck fighting traffic all day. But then I'm placed in a conversation with someone and get a chance to make him smile. It's like the Lord sent me there. I don't take credit for the opportunity or the results. I'm just doing what the Lord would have me to do.

I've been blessed to be on the *Duck Dynasty* series. I don't think it happened by chance. I know it came from the Lord above. So I see it as an opportunity to speak to others about God—to help them be aware of why they're on this earth.

I don't think we should hold in all the wisdom we have from the Lord. We need to go out into the world and deliver it. Spread the Word. Give back. Just like the Blues Brothers, we're on a mission from God. But our mission is to go out in the world and spread the Word. There's no better feeling than to see the opportunities God provides and to do the Lord's work.

I don't get invited to many churches. Most of my events are custom car shows, expos, hockey games, baseball games, and other outdoor events. I take whatever opportunity they give me to encourage folk. I try to put the Lord first. A lot of people come to me and say, "Thank you for making a godly show that our kids can watch."

It gives me an opportunity to say, "Thank you. We're just doing what God leads us to do."

Planting seeds for me is taking the opportunity to share a quick part of my story, give some advice about a practical matter, or just listen. This is what works for me. But you have to figure out what's going to work for you.

When You Find Hard Soil

Some of the people I talk to don't understand what *Duck Dynasty* is about. They think we long-haired bearded fellows like to drink alcohol or do drugs. But who we are on the show is who we are in private. When I share this with them, sometimes they're disappointed. But then I look off in the distance and see someone give me a thumbs-up. Or after I share a truth I feel God wants me to suggest to them, they'll say, "That's the same thing my brother-in-law was telling me. I should probably listen." My job is just to speak the truth in love.

Sometimes the conversation or activity gets out of hand.

When that happens, I'll change the subject, talk to somebody else, or just walk away if I need to. Once you have the power of the Holy Spirit inside, those temptations aren't as hard to turn away from. The Holy Spirit puts words in my mouth so I know what seeds to sow. I often don't know what I'm going to say or how I'll respond, but because I want to follow the Lord, he helps me.

Some people still just don't get your mission. I was in Ohio doing an event and there was a family who came to talk with me. They told me they lived on a farm and they had a daughter with them. She was a very pretty little girl. She said, "Mountain Man, can I ask you something? Would you go out with me?"

I said, "Little girl, how old are you?"

"I'm fifteen."

"Well, if I could put myself in a time machine and go back forty years, I would, but I'm afraid you're just a little too young for me."

I think her mom and dad were upset with me. Maybe they thought I was a millionaire and just wanted their daughter to hook up with someone successful. But that wouldn't work for me.

Planting seeds takes some good soil and good watering. Before I start my day, or before an event, I like to go into a quiet room and get on my knees and say a prayer to guide me through this mission I'm on. People can't figure out what I'm doing.

They wonder, "Where'd Mountain Man go?"

"He's in a room."

"What's he doing in there?"

Prayer releases God's rain that makes the ground ready for the seeds, and also waters the seeds he wants to grow and bear fruit.

John 15:4 says,

> *Abide in Me, and I in you. As the branch can-*
> *not bear fruit of itself, unless it abides in the vine,*
> *neither can you, unless you abide in Me.*

Keepin' a slow profile means that you take time to abide in the vine—spend time with God. You can't bear good fruit on your own unless you're connected to God and let the seeds of his Word into your heart.

You can also help others by planting good seeds in their lives. What kind of seeds are you planting with your character? Sow good seeds by being a good example, and look for opportunities to sow seeds with the unique way God made you.

8

Do It Right the First Time

One time I went to a house to work on an air conditioner. Air-conditioning units are usually on the outside so I just got to fixing the unit, getting the Freon right, and cleaning it. When I got done, I knocked on the front door.

A lady answered and I said, "I got your air going. It's in good shape now."

She said, "Thank you, Sonny, for doing that."

"Well, this is what I charge..."

"But I didn't call an air-conditioning man."

I had fixed the wrong air conditioner. The one I was supposed to fix was next door. I guess I got a little mixed up. The lady was appreciative and offered me some cookies. But I was running behind time. I made sure to check the house number the next time to make sure I was working on the right air conditioner.

I like to get the job done right the first time. I usually do because I work a little slower. If you slow down and make sure you're doing the job right, you won't have come back and look like you didn't know what you were doing. That's not good for business. Most people would rather have you slow down just a bit and get it right.

Doing it right the first time really paid off for me in the air-conditioning business. I usually did my work in the morning while it was still cool in the attic. If I was called back because of a problem, it would likely be 120 degrees up there.

Do the extra it takes to make sure the job is done right. You're less likely to get a nasty call from a customer using words that aren't used in church. Bosses only tolerate so many errors, and your business loses money when you have to go out again. So slow down. Pay attention to details. Get stuff out of the way so you can focus. Double check so you don't have to redo it later.

Value Hard Work

Hard work makes you stronger in life and more able to deal with what's ahead of you. Preschool gets you ready for kindergarten. Kindergarten prepares you for first grade. And so on. Hard work gets you ready for life no matter what you do. No one is going to hand you life on a silver platter. You need to experience it for yourself. Some people don't get their first job until after college. If you wait until then to experience what it's like to do hard work, you'll likely go through several jobs before figuring out what real work is like.

Start building your resume at an early age by learning how to set goals for your day, working hard, and getting things done with a good attitude. That's what employers are looking for. And you want to build a good resume for the Lord.

Stick with the Plan

As I've gotten older, I've learned what works best for me. I try to have a plan of approach for what I do each day so that I can stick with what works and get it right the first time. Then I don't go into every situation guessing.

Be careful not to change up what's already working for you. Plan your attack and stick with your plan. If something comes to your mind that works better and can help you get it done faster, add that in. But if you're constantly making sudden random changes, you'll make more mistakes. I've found that good preparation, sticking with a proven plan, and timely follow-through works best.

Be Friendly, but Avoid Distractions

I used to run into distractions all the time. Little old ladies were the worst. Actually they were the best because they kept bringing me food, cake, and cookies. But that was the worst distraction. They tried to put five pounds on me before I left. Sometimes I would do more eating than working because I didn't want to turn down the food. I'm a big eater. I think they were waiting for someone to feed and I was all for it!

One lady fed me so much that before I knew it, I got sleepy and started to fall asleep in her chair.

I heard her say, "Oh, it's nap time. I like to take naps too."

"Yes, Ma'am. I'm getting sleepy. Whoa, I'd better get back to work."

"Well, I got some more cake back here."

"Oh, thank you, Ma'am. That's really nice of you."

Other times kids want to show me their toys. The toys these days are pretty neat. One time I forgot what I was doing and the mom found me playing with her kid and his toys. She scolded him.

I apologized and said, "That's the neatest little remote control car I've seen in a while. He's not bothering me."

Kids always wanted to know what all my tools and instruments were. Sometimes I showed them the voltmeter. I said, "Here, hold this," and they got a little shock.

There's a time to be friendly, and there's a time to get your work done. Eliminate those distractions, even if they're delicious and fun! If you're trying to do something and someone turns on the TV or is making a bunch of noise, say, "Hey, I can't study." Or maybe you just need to go somewhere else to get your work done. Don't just accept it and do nothing. Make a change.

Stay Positive

A negative attitude creates resistance and slows me down in the wrong way. A positive attitude reduces resistance to allow me to think clearly and quickly so I can do good work.

The best way to stay positive is to start your day with a good outlook. Wake up, stretch real good, say a good prayer, open the curtain, look outside and say, "Hey it's another great day on planet Earth." Some people didn't wake up this morning. But you and I did. Thank the Lord for that!

After that I let my dog out and cook me up some breakfast. My dog is always glad to see me. I also like to throw out some sunflower seeds for the squirrels. I like to have fat squirrels around me so if Armageddon comes and Bruce Willis doesn't save the world, I'll have a bunch of fat squirrels to eat.

Sometimes I watch a little TV if I have some time. It's tough to turn on the TV and find good news, so I like to watch *The Andy Griffith Show*, *Gunsmoke*, or *Bonanza*. Cheerful things on the TV help your day stay positive.

I believe you can find something positive in everything. You just need to shake out the negative and see what's left. Negativity doesn't get anyone anywhere but a bad place. It just grows and becomes overwhelming. I have to keep a positive attitude or I don't think straight and don't feel right with God.

My daddy used to say, "There is always someone really smart who can do something really well. Maybe you can't do it as well as they can, but I bet you can do part of it." This taught me to always assume I have a chance of succeeding and to work with a positive attitude to contribute what I can.

This attitude helps me to work hard and do it right the first time. No matter how difficult the task, I know God can help me figure out a way to move that mountain. I believe God will help you move that mountain too.

I think Colossians 3:23–24 says it right:

> *And whatever you do, do it heartily, as to the*
> *Lord and not to men, knowing that from the*
> *Lord you will receive the reward of the*
> *inheritance; for you serve the Lord Christ.*

Did you know that if you're a Christian you're a servant of Christ? As a servant of the Lord, do your work as unto him. He's a great boss and loves you no matter what.

That doesn't mean you should slack off. Value hard work. Slow down and do it right the first time. Have a plan and stick with it. Avoid distractions and stay postive. If you do that, you can be sure that you'll receive a reward from the Lord.

9

Pray on Your Knees

I was hunting on the first day of bow season. It had been raining and the creek was higher than normal. All day I waited up in a tree with my crossbow, but never saw a deer. I climbed down the tree, jumped the creek, and started walking uphill back to my truck about a half-mile away. I saw some turnips on the ground and could see where some hogs had rooted them up.

It was getting dark so I got out my Walmart flashlight with two D batteries inside. I shined the light up ahead and heard some noises. It wasn't a deer. I heard an animal squeal and thought, *It's a wild hog. That's not good.*

I moved closer thinking I could get a shot at the hog—not to bring home for supper, but to keep from being eaten for supper. The sow came rushing at me and I shined the light right in its eye. I thought she was going to attack me, but the light stopped her from charging. Boy, I was shaking all over, especially when I realized there was more than one hog.

I was preparing for the worst. Thoughts were rushing through my head. *How in the world can I shoot this hog in the dark, re-cock the bow, and stick another arrow in for the next shot?* I wasn't going to say, "Hey you angry sows. I know I just shot your buddy, but could those of you who are still alive just hold up a second while I reload and shoot?" I've always heard that if you shoot one and it's squealing, the others will come and attack you. These hogs have been known to kill people and eat them.

I had a pretty good lock-blade pocketknife in my pocket. *I'm going to get one shot at this. Should I aim for the head, or will it ricochet off? Maybe I should stick it in the neck. Am I going to end up in hand-to-hand combat, knife-jabbing this hog?*

Finally the hog went off and appeared to be headed in the same direction I was. The ground was muddy—*squish-squash* all the way. I couldn't run and there were no trees to climb. I couldn't see that hog any more, but I heard the others nearby and could smell them.

I thought, *I got to get to my truck. I'm the only one out here.* I walked a little further and realized that I was up against two sows with their litters. They were taking turns charging at me. I tried retreating and acting like I was scared, and then they really came at me. I prayed. Then I tried to be aggressive and that made them even madder. I prayed some more. I tried singing to the hogs. But they just carried on chomping their teeth, grunting, drooling, and running around squealing here and there. I wasn't doing anything to them. I just wanted to get in my truck and get out of there.

The mamas just got madder. After being charged at twelve to fifteen times, I finally got upwind so they couldn't smell me. But the piglets had gotten into some thickets and could still sense where I was. So here came Piggly, Wiggly, Squiggly, and the rest of them piglets, running right underneath my feet, squalling as loud as they could. They were just acting dumb. I could have grabbed them if I wanted to. Their mama came charging one more time but didn't get quite as close as before.

I reached my truck and hopped up in the back shouting, "All right! Where you hogs at now? I'm going to kill every one of you!" But they were gone.

My stomach hurt so bad. It was knotted up with tension. I suppose it goes without saying that during this whole experience I was praying to God. I think prayer is the only thing that got me out.

I make prayer a daily part of my life. I pray before I get in the deer stand that I don't fall out. I pray for my son. I pray for people I know. I try to keep prayer in my life and I think the good Lord is looking out after me, especially out in the woods with a bunch of angry hogs.

Use Your Knees to Get Close to God

Prayer is something you can do anytime, anywhere. You can pray in the shower, in your car, on your bed, at the mall. You can walk, sit, run, or lie down when you pray. But I like to pray on my knees. I feel that praying on my knees puts more devotion into my prayers. It's an outward sign of how weak I am compared to the Almighty. There's no other object or person that I would get on my knees for except God. He's the only one. When I kneel, it's like my prayer gets out there quicker. It probably all goes out the same way, but when I'm on my knees, I'm calling out in urgency and showing respect for the Master.

Don't just say a little ol' prayer and wait for a miracle. I want to encourage you to get down on your hands and knees. There's a good chance the Lord himself won't just show up and say, "Come on, I'm going to take you by the hand and lead you out." But God will use people and circumstances to show you the way.

I was once the grand marshal at a strawberry festival in Portland, Tennessee. We were about halfway through the parade when my driver got a phone call. As I was waving at all the people, I looked over and noticed something didn't seem right and said, "Joey, what's wrong?"

He said, "Something's happened to Mama. They're rushing her to the emergency room right now."

I said, "Oh my goodness," and immediately started to pray while continuing to wave to the crowd. As we went along, I kept looking over at Joey asking, "Are you okay? You okay?"

He said, "Yeah, yeah, I'll be all right." I'm sure he was upset, even wanting to cry. But what could he do? We were stuck in the middle of the parade with a police car in front of us leading the way and a good twenty-five thousand people around us on the parade route.

Joey got on the phone and called the officer who sped up a little bit when he heard the news. We were going by pretty quick waving at people. At the end of the route we were supposed to turn around and come back slowly. But the policeman said, "I'm going to clear the way for you, Joey, where you can go back to your truck and get on up to the hospital."

And, boy, we zoomed right up to his truck. We got out and Joey went to talk to some people. I went behind an old truck and got down on my knees to pray.

Joey and his wife saw me and came over to where I was, asking, "Tim, what's wrong?"

I said, "Everything's okay with me. I was just praying for your mama."

"Well, thank you" Joey said. "I appreciate you doing that." He told me that he had just talked to his brother who told him their mama was going to be okay.

I'm glad that I took the time to pray. We don't always know the effect our prayers have. But the Bible says in James 5:16, "The effective, fervent prayer of a righteous man avails much." I believe that the prayers we pray as God's children are powerful. So keeping praying, and try praying on your knees.

Pray It Out and Trust God's Plan

Some people have good ideas, but others give bad advice. Don't jump into a decision too quickly. Slow down and wait on the Lord. Weigh both sides. Think about what they're saying. Say, "I'm going to go home and pray about it tonight and I'll give you my decision in the morning." If it's something that can wait, I keep praying about it. I find that I make better decisions when I pray sincerely for God's wisdom.

You don't have to go through life not knowing what to do. God has a plan for you and he wants you to ask him about it. Without prayer, it may never come to pass. Don't think God's just going to show you the way no matter how you're living. The enemy has a plan too. That's why you need to pray. Be patient for God's answer. Maybe it's not your time for the plan to come to you quite yet. Slow down, wait, and trust. God has a plan cooking in the oven just for you.

Each morning I thank the Lord for what he's done and then pray something like this: "Heavenly Father, thank you for another day on the earth. I pray today that I'll do what you want me to do. Show me your way. I want to serve you. Only you, Lord, can guide me. Lead me and I will do my best."

Ask God to Fill Your Mouth

The highlight of my week is usually doing my radio show. (Hey, be sure to tune in each Tuesday afternoon at 5 p.m. Central. Check out the About the Author page at the back of this book for station and call-in information along with how you can listen or stream video online.) I walk in with my Bible and a verse I want to read on the air, and I pray for the Lord to fill my mouth with the right words as I talk to the fans who call in.

Don't fill up your mouth with a bunch of worldly garbage. Ask the Lord what you should say. Ask him to fill you up with what he's give you to speak. People don't realize that our mouths commit the worst sins. Luke 6:45 records these words of Jesus:

> A good man out of the good treasure of his heart brings forth good; and an evil man out of the evil treasure of his heart brings forth evil. For out of the abundance of the heart his mouth speaks.

Some people just spit out their words and don't even know what they're saying. I've asked people, "Why'd you say that?"

They've said back to me, "I never said that." But they did. People don't know what they say half the time and don't realize how much garbage comes out. Think about your words before you let them out. Don't speak hastily. Slow down and make the words of Psalm 19:14 your prayer:

Let the words of my mouth and the meditation of
  my heart
Be acceptable in Your sight, O Lord, my strength
  and my Redeemer.

If you can talk slower than you think, you have it made. I get the privilege of meeting lots of people all the time. I pray for the Lord to fill my mouth with the right words. When someone asks me a question, I pause and listen. Before I share, I say a sincere prayer asking the Lord to give me words of wisdom. I don't jump right into it. I analyze it and let it sink in, and then the answer flows out of me. It's kind of like I'm not the one doing the talking even though I am. The power of the Lord is helping me to speak.

I'm not an ordained minister and I know I'm not the smartest guy in the world. But when I talk to people, I don't worry about my answers and they come out right. People get the point when I answer the way God wants me to. Talking slow helps. I think fast and can have a lot of things running through my head before I say the next word. I seldom freeze up unless I'm really tired. If I don't say anything, sometimes I'm just waiting in prayer for the wisdom to come from the Lord.

What About Unanswered Prayer?

Sometimes things don't work out the way we want and it looks like God isn't listening. Some people call that unanswered prayer. Thank God for what you feel are unanswered prayers. Sometimes the prayer has been answered but we don't know it until later in life. Sometimes God is in the process of answering that prayer. It's just not going to happen right then. Sometimes God has a different answer. God is not slow like we understand slowness. But he is patient and does what he's going to do in his time and in his way for his good purpose. God keeps a slow profile for a reason, and he wants you to slow down and pray.

KEEPIN' A SLOW PROFILE

There's a real simple Bible verse in 1 Thessalonians 5:17. It says, "Pray without ceasing." Well, that's pretty easy to understand. Emm hmmm. When you pray, get on your knees and honor the Lord. You can trust him to take care of you. You don't have to worry. Philippians 4:6–7 says,

> *Be anxious for nothing, but in everything by prayer and supplication, with thanksgiving, let your requests be made known to God; and the peace of God, which surpasses all understanding, will guard your hearts and minds through Christ Jesus.*

Did you know that God wants to fill your mouth with good words? Listen to what the Holy Spirit says to you through prayer. God wants to use your voice in this world. Talk slower than you think and God will fill your mouth with words of life to share with others.

10

Get Along with Others

When I lived in Tennessee, I knew an old man who was very grumpy. No one came around his house. Everything he said was obnoxious. I was really nice to him and tried everything I could think of to cheer him up. One time I shot a bottle rocket up in the air. It accidentally went down his overalls and blew up. That sure didn't cheer up him up right then, but he laughed about it later.

I was at his house one day and he started his negative talk. I said, "You know, you're the grumpiest old man I've ever met. What's your problem? Did you step in dog poo this morning? I don't blame those others for not wanting to come around here." Well, it started out rough and he got mad at me, but I got him to laugh and broke through his shell. No one had stood up to him before. He just had some issues and got tired of people trying to be nice to him. We got to be pretty good friends.

Some of my good friends today were once grumpy. People

just got mad and cussed at them. I decided to aggravate them a bit until I'd get a laugh out of them. "Is your nose really like that or have you been in a closed-up chicken coop all day?"

I got along well with old timers, especially the grumpy ones. They liked me even though I didn't listen to their moaning and groaning.

Don't Treat Everyone the Same

One of my elementary school teachers told me, "There aren't two people who are the same, and sometimes you can't figure out a person." I learned that you may have to change your approach to communicating with them, or responding to their actions.

It's important to treat everyone well. Be the same person you are, but handle others uniquely. They're not robots; they're human beings made in God's image. It's always good to just slow down, listen to them first, and know where they're really coming from. Get a little wisdom about what's going on before jumping in. Then you can have a plan on how to talk with them so you can get along with them.

Forgive Quickly and Often

When I was about fourteen years old, some of my buddies jumped on me and worked me over. I think they jumped me out of jealousy because I could out-shoot them in the woods. But I'm not sure and they never told me. They didn't beat me up too bad, and I got some good licks on them. You'd think that I wouldn't trust them after that. But I didn't hold a grudge and still talk to them today.

All my life I've never been able to hold a grudge. It's just not in me. That's a good thing because God doesn't want us to hold sins against each other. I don't believe we're living right before the Lord if we're holding a grudge. If anyone should have a grudge, it should be Jesus Christ for what they did to him. But Jesus forgave them. I feel holding a grudge is sinful. It's certainly not helpful. Grudges act like negativity in your life. They not only affect that one relationship, but the others in your life too.

When bad things happen, our first response is usually anger, hurt, and disappointment. We can't believe someone did this to us and it's hard to let it go. If you're holding a grudge against someone, I have just one question for you: Are you holding the grudge or is the grudge holding you? There's a good chance that person doesn't even think about you or the thing that happened that's so important to you. So in reality, the grudge is holding you. Turn it over to the Lord and let it go. God will take care of it and you'll be happier.

I've heard the expression "forgive and forget." You must forgive if you want to live clean in your emotions and not be haunted by your hurts. But I don't think you should forget. Forgiving is like getting stung by a bee. You let God take out the stinger, but you remember where that hive is so you don't make the same mistake twice.

Romans 12:17–21 gives some pretty good advice about how to get along well with others.

> Repay no one evil for evil. Have regard for good things in the sight of all men. If it is possible, as much as depends on you, live peaceably with all men. Beloved, do not avenge yourselves, but *rather* give place to wrath; for it is written, "Vengeance *is* Mine, I will repay," says the Lord. Therefore "If your enemy is hungry, feed him; If he is thirsty, give him a drink; For in so doing you will heap coals of fire on his head." Do not be overcome by evil, but overcome evil with good.

Be Yourself

When I was about twenty, I worked for an electrical company. My supervisor was a Vietnam army veteran and a really a tough egg to get along with. He was as redneck as they come. People didn't like him too well, but he really thought I was different. He admired the way I talked and I amused him.

We got to be really good friends. He thought the world of me and taught me how to do electrical work. He got to like me and would do anything for me. Treated me with kindness.

I took the time to be with him and talked to him. He needed someone to talk to. If I had a date, I would call the date off—it wasn't much of a date anyway. He and I drove the country roads and looked at groundhogs out in the fields. He couldn't believe how much I loved to hunt. I'd jump out of the truck to kill a squirrel. He was always talking about how hungry I was. "You eat more than anyone I've ever seen."

He liked me because of the things that make me unique—my voice, mannerisms, appetite, love for squirrel hunting. If I wasn't myself, he wouldn't have liked me. There were enough people around to prove that. To get along with people it's important to be yourself. If you're not yourself, who are they liking? Someone else.

Not too long ago a school principal came up to me and said, "You've started an epidemic in my school. All I hear down my hallways is 'Emm hmmm.' In the classrooms, 'Emm hmmm.' A kid will say, 'I'm going to get me a grape slushy when I get out of school. Emm hmmm.'"

I told him, "I'm sorry about that."

He said, "No, we love you Mountain Man."

I imagine a lot of those kids get in trouble during roll call. "Johnny, are you here?"

"Emm hmmm."

I never would have guessed that just being myself would have gotten me this far in life. Be yourself. It'll help you get along with others, and it'll help you get along in life.

Take Off the Blinders

The key to getting along with other people is vision. You have to be aware of your surroundings and have a wide angle look on life and not have tunnel vision, seeing just what's in front of you.

Look around. Observe people. Sometimes you see things that might catch your attention. Don't be a mule with blinders only seeing one perspective. Take those blinders off and look around. See things. Someone is next to you with a need and you're not noticing.

I once saw an older guy at the side of a four-lane divided highway. He was probably about seventy-five years old and he reminded me of my dad. I stopped and asked, "Sir, are you having problems?"

"I can't get my car to start." I fiddled around a little bit under the hood but couldn't get the car to start either. He asked, "Can you take me up near the mall?" We drove over to the mall and looked for one of his relatives. I eventually connected him with a police officer who said he'd be happy to help.

How many times do we just drive past people in need? I'm not saying you need to stop for everyone. Be safe. Just pay attention and ask the Lord what you should do. I was grateful to help that man get the help he needed.

When I used to go into people's houses, I ended up doing more than just fixing their air-conditioning. Sometimes I helped them move some furniture or find something that was lost. I grabbed their mail and rolled their garbage can in. Not only were they grateful, they wanted me to come back and work for them.

By slowing down I can see how I can help people. Helping people gives me a good feeling and honors the Lord. It also builds trust and a good relationship for the future.

I love getting along with others. It's what God has for me to do.

KEEPIN' A SLOW PROFILE

Romans 2:4 says that it's the goodness or kindness of God that leads people to repentance. Sometimes people think that in order to help someone come to the Lord you need to tell them how sinful they are. I think this Bible verse has a good strategy for leading people to the Lord—kindness.

Kindness takes time. Slow down so you can see the people God's pointing out to you.

Be careful not to treat everyone the same. You are unique and so is everyone else. Be yourself and look for ways you can get along with others. Be sure to forgive when you get hurt. It's just not worth it to hold onto a grudge.

Who do you know that could use some kindness from God? Think about what you can do to make a difference.

11

Get a Good Dog

My daddy had a lot of rat terriers growing up. He loved this breed of dog. They are really lovable and make great pets. Plus the dog will hunt just about anything you train it to hunt. So guess what kind of dog we had when I was growing up? Yep. Rat terriers.

When we moved to Tennessee, Daddy got us one. We called him Rep.

Rep

Rep got distemper when he was a puppy. Distemper is a viral disease that's deadly. We didn't think he was going to live through it. He lived, but his back right paw twitched all the time, even when he slept.

Rep wanted to go everywhere we went. We used to take him frog hunting. We'd be out in the boat at night shining the light on frogs trying to be quiet. All we could hear was *bump,*

bump-bump, bump, bump of Rep's leg twitching against the metal seat. A duck would swim by and down in the water he went. We'd shine the light out there and see the ducks fleeing from Rep with Rep about twenty feet behind them.

One of us would say, "There he is. He'll be back in a little while." We kept frog hunting and sooner or later he'd come back to the boat and jump in. Rep was a loyal companion.

When Daddy woke up each morning, Rep would meet him. Daddy would get the newspaper from outside and Rep would do his business. After about a month of watching Daddy get the paper, Rep did his business and got the newspaper on the way back in. So Daddy started to say, "Rep, go get the newspaper," and Rep would do his business, grab the paper, and run inside.

We didn't have stuffed animals growing up. We had Rep. He would sleep with us and was a great watchdog. Some people have cats, but I prefer a dog. I can see why a dog is called a man's best friend.

For fun we kids used to jump off a bridge into the water. It was about twenty feet up and the water was six feet deep. You had to make a quick cut after you hit the water so you didn't smack the bottom and get hurt. I used to do a one-and-a-half-turn flip off the bridge. Don't try that at home, please.

Well, ol' Rep saw us and wanted to do the same. One day he jumped up on my leg like he was trying to get my attention, so I grabbed him and threw him off the bridge into the water. He loved it. He swam to an old tree that had fallen with roots still in the water and climbed back up to where we were. He hopped on the ledge and we threw him off again. He took that twenty-foot drop and *whoosh*. He swam to the shore and got back up to the bridge. We threw him off time after time. We had to stop because we knew he had to catch his breath. He just kept going. He loved the water.

Whatever we wanted to hunt—rabbit, quail, dove, squirrel—Rep would be by our side. He would retrieve anything for us.

Rep didn't like cats. The neighbor had a litter of kittens. There were a lot of them and they ran wild. We stored a lot of clothes in our garage to take to Louisiana to give to Ordy Mae for all her kids. The kittens got into the garage and urinated on them. We just had to throw them away. The neighbor had no control and couldn't catch those cats to get rid of them.

Then suddenly the cats just disappeared.

One day we were out digging for worms in a field in back of our house. Guess what we found: cat skulls and bones. We could never say Rep done it, but we had a good idea Rep was smart enough to get rid of the evidence.

About four years after we got Rep, he got hit by a car in the street. His leg finally quit twitching. I was about twelve years old when he died. It was heartbreaking. His death tore me to pieces. If they have dogs in heaven, I'm sure Rep is there.

Nubs

After Rep we got another rat terrier and named him Nubs. Nubs loved to swim just like Rep. We threw him off the bridge too.

Nubs loved being on the dock with us as we fished. If we weren't watching our poles and one started to bend, Nubs would start barking so we knew to reel in the catfish. He was like an alarm dog.

Nubs wasn't as good a hunter as Rep, but he was a good loving dog. He didn't like cats either, but no cats went missing. One day he just didn't come home. We think someone stole him. His departure was easier than seeing Rep get run over. Not much, but a little better. We still missed ol' Nubs.

Radar

Our last dog was Radar—another rat terrier. He was the best watchdog of all of them. He kept his ears down, but if he heard a noise, his ears would go straight up like radar and he would bark.

Radar got run over by a car too and went off to find a place to die. My brother followed the blood trail across a field to an old abandoned shack. Radar was under the house, but Bill saw that his leg was broken and his paw was bleeding. We got him to a pet hospital and they had to amputate one of his toes. After that he always limped with that leg. But he lived!

I used to put Radar under my coat and take him for a ride on my Honda P50. He peeked out of the coat and barked at everything. People were amused at the kid driving down the street holding onto a barking dog.

I could tell you about a few other dogs, but these were my favorite growing up.

A dog helps me relax better than many humans. They're always happy and just want to show you love. What a wonderful gift. That loving atmosphere relieves you of the things that are bothering you.

If you have a good dog, take some time each day to spend loving it. It relieves tension. It really does. And you'll make some good memories for years to come. Don't throw them off a bridge, though, unless they really like it.

Do you have a pet that you love? Caring for my dogs has helped me to slow down and focus on what's really important—friendship.
Proverbs 18:24 says,

> *A man who has friends must himself be friendly,*
> *But there is a friend who sticks closer than a*
> *brother.*

I love my brother Bill. He's been a close friend. And so have my dogs. They've shown me how to show myself friendly. Friendship is important and I want to be friendly to others. What does friendship mean to you? Do something today to show yourself friendly.

12

God Is Your Flashlight

One morning when Jonathan was about seven years old, we decided to go hunting. We got out into the woods and starting looking for squirrels. We got separated and soon I heard three shots, which was his signal to me that he was lost. It had started to rain and everything was wet, including our three-wheeler. When I went to yank on the pull cord to start the engine, my hand slipped and the mechanism snapped back. One of my fingers hurt real bad and I knew that it was busted up.

I used my other hand to crank the engine and went to find Jonathan. We had walkie-talkies so I said, "Shoot again." I finally found him and we headed to the emergency room. The doctor did an X-ray, which showed the bone was splintered and turned around backwards.

All the doctor could do at that moment was put a splint on it. He said, "You're going to have to have an operation."

I said, "Okay, put a splint on it." When he finished, we

headed back out to the woods. This time I said, "Son, don't wander off the trail too far. Stay along the levee where the trail is so you don't get lost." But he got out of my sight and soon I heard three shots. *Oh no, not again.*

It had gotten real foggy and was getting dark. We had the radios, but each time he shot, I couldn't tell where the sound was coming from. I made such a zigzag trail trying to find Jonathan, that when I finally got to him, I couldn't remember the trail out.

We hopped on the three-wheeler together. It was dark and everything looked the same. As we slowly wove through the trees, the three-wheeler wouldn't idle so the engine kept cutting out. Everything went pitch black, and I tried to restart the engine. It cranked up and we went on our way a bit more before the engine cut out again. This time the pull cord broke when I tried to start it.

Everything was quiet and dark. We had no flashlight. There was no moon, no stars, and a misty fog was filling the woods. Jonathan wanted to cry, but I'd been lost so many times in the woods at night that I reassured him everything was going to be okay. We tried to push-start the three-wheeler, but the ground was muddy and the wheels only slid across the ground no matter what gear we tried.

So I said, "We're going to have to leave the three-wheeler here and try to get out of these woods on foot." I had a small lighter in my pocket for making fires. I lit it up and noticed we had entered a little ravine. I thought it was odd to find this little gully in the flat woods. Now those little lighters get so hot that they'll burn your hand. So I had it lit for only a short time, then we walked in the darkness. You couldn't even see your hand if it was in front of your face.

I had my cell phone, but there was no reception where we were. I thought, *This is bad*. We kept walking, holding our hands in front of our faces to protect our eyes from the low-hanging branches. We heard animals running around and Jonathan was trying to keep from crying. I said, "Son, I know we're alone and it's scary. But we got each other here and we got God. We're going to get out of this thing." He calmed right down.

I figured we'd have to wait until daylight. I started using my lighter again, feeling around for tree branches with leaves. I broke some off a tree and made a little bed for Jonathan and me. We lay down for a little while, but it was warm enough outside for snakes to be crawling around. I said, "Maybe we ought to just try to walk out of here."

So I pulled out my lighter again for a quick look around. A few minutes later we ran into a stream. I could feel it trickling under my feet. I said, "Well, I don't know how deep this water is or how far it goes, but let's walk a little farther, Son." We had rubber boots on and the water started to get deeper.

Then I heard a *plop* in front of me—a sound I'd heard many times before. It was a snake rolling off a low-hanging tree limb into the water. I said, "Son, I think we need to go the other way." So we kept walking, probably for two hours.

I lit the lighter to see which way the mist was falling. This helped to guide our direction because we still had no stars or moon. Finally the lighter gave out and we had no light.

I'd been trying my phone from time to time, praying for a signal, and I finally got ahold of a friend. He knew the area we were in and knew where I'd parked. So he drove to the parking lot and started honking his horn. It was so good to talk on the cell to someone. We'd walk a little ways and I'd tell him to honk again. He'd honk. We zigzagged toward the horn because it echoed like a gunshot did.

It took about an hour after he first started honking the horn for us to get out of there. Being lost twice in one day is kind of rough. We just kept praying, "God, get us out of here," and God got us out of the woods. But it was a real scary experience and we didn't come back with any squirrels.

The moral of the story is if you're going to go hunting in the evening, make sure you have a flashlight in your pocket. But if you don't have a flashlight, pray. I just feel that if you keep praying, God is going to get you out of trouble one way or another. He's going to be that guiding light for you even if you don't have any light of your own.

Jonathan and I got lost another time at night in the woods. This time we were deer hunting. I stopped and built a little pallet of branches to lie on because it was wet on the ground. The sky was clear and Jonathan and I were lying on the mat of leaves looking up at the stars. I was praying, "Lord, get us out of here. Please get us out."

We continued to look up and one of the stars seemed to shine brighter than the others. There was a sapling nearby and I rolled under it, hiding the bright star. The bright star moved so that it was again in sight. I thought, *Did I just see that star move?*

So I rolled to the other side of the tree so the star was hidden again. The star went to the other side. I did this two or three times and Jonathan started to wonder what I was doing.

I said, "Son, look at the bright star. You see the one I'm pointing at?"

He said, "Yeah, Daddy, I see it."

I said, "Roll back in here."

Jonathan said, "Daddy, it moved."

I said, "Yeah, sure did. Let's do it again." So we rolled back and forth a few times watching the star follow us. I said, "This is very odd."

"Daddy," he said, "you think I ought to point my gun at it and see what it does?"

I said, "No, no, no. I don't know what that is up there. What if it's a flying saucer or something and they shoot us with a ray gun? We'd better not do that." I don't know what it was, but we played games with the star until we got tired. Then we decided to try to get out of the woods but couldn't find our four-wheeler. So I called a friend who came to pick us up.

I got lost another time by myself in the dark with no light (you'd think I'd learn my lesson). This time I was on a game reserve on Halloween night with coyotes chasing me. I had a crossbow with me and got away. It seems like God always has his hands on me. He guides me through all these adventures.

Sometimes things get gloomy and I can't see well. God gives me a light to see with. Without his light we're going to get off his path. I've been lost in the woods without a flashlight. I don't want to be lost in life without his light. But if you do get lost—in the woods or in life—don't ever give up. God will show you the light. God is my light. He's the light of my life.

Daddy and Mama Knew Their Bible

My daddy is ninety years old as this book is getting ready to be published and he knows his Bible from front to back. He knew it back when I was a kid too. When I was a rascal, he didn't spare the rod. He knew that Bible verse for sure.
He often read something out of the Bible to me that he was going to use in his Sunday school class. He'd say, "Here's something you might want to read, Tim." I enjoyed the stories of David killing Goliath, Samson getting his hair cut (well, I didn't like that part), Jonah and the big fish, and when Jesus multiplied a few fish to feed thousands of people.

I remember him reading a story to me about some she-bears. You probably aren't going to hear about this one in Sunday school. Some youths were calling the prophet Elisha names because of his bald head. Elisha didn't like it and cursed them. Two female bears came out of the woods and mauled all forty-two youths. That'll teach you to make fun of the prophet. Emm hmmm.

My dad still gives me Bible verses to read on my own and for my radio show.

My mom kept her Bible by her bed and I saw her reading it every day. She wanted us to do God's work and do good.

Moms and dads, read your Bible yourselves and also to your kids. Psalm 119:105 says, "Your word is a lamp to my feet and a light to my path." God's word is our flashlight if we'll shine it out in front of us.

Pick Up Your Bible

Sometimes I catch myself in a flurry of phone calls, text messages, newscasters reporting all that's wrong in the world, people with problems…and I just stop. It's time to slow down and grab my Bible. I'll open it and thumb around to find what God has for me. As I read, a soothing force comes over me. It's a great feeling taking twenty to thirty minutes in the Bible. The world's not going to blow up. I can let everything else wait.

Some people ask me, "Mountain Man, why are you so calm?"

I say, "Why for $20 I'll tell you. Got a Bible? Pick it up. I'll take a rain check on that $20 or you can pay me right now."

Don't let anyone pile a bunch of stuff on top of your Bible so you can't find it. There are so many lessons you can learn from the Bible.

Not too long ago someone close to me died. I couldn't understand it. I wanted to know why. It's hard when someone close to you dies and you're still alive. We want answers. God's Word has answers for us.

Whenever there's a problem, I figure out what's bothering me the most and then I have a personal Bible study to find verses that pertain to that situation. Sometimes it takes a while, but in the process I learn about other things in the Bible. When I first started reading my Bible consistently, I could open my Bible and find the answer right in front of me. I thought I could do that all the time, but it doesn't work like that. I'm not a magician and God's not Santa Claus.

God wants me to read more so I can learn more about the Bible and what he's like. I read the verses and ask God what I'm supposed to do. He always helps me hit the nail on the head by helping me to find exactly what I need to read.

Nighttime is the best time for me to read the Bible. Time in the Word just settles me down from the stress of the day. When you get stressed out and are wandering around in the darkness, pick up your Bible. God will be your flashlight day or night, giving you exactly what you need. It works for me every single time.

When you feel like you're lost and there's no way out, ask God to come in to guide you and show you his path out. The first step to keepin' the slow profile that God has for you is to invite him into your life. The Bible says that we have all sinned and the penalty for our sin is death. But God has given us a free gift of salvation that we can accept. The Bible says that all who call upon the name of the Lord will be saved.

Jesus once said, "I am the light of the world. He who follows me shall not walk in darkness, but have the light of life." Do you need his light? If you do, call upon him right now. Pray this little prayer with me:

> Heavenly Father, thank you for giving me the opportunity to live on this earth. Thank you for sending your only Son Jesus Christ to die for my sins so that I can have eternal life with you. Father, I've sinned. Jesus, forgive me and wash me clean. Fill me with your Spirit and your power. I want to follow in your footsteps every day of my life. Help me to slow down enough to be a blessing to those around me. In Jesus' name, amen.

If you just invited Jesus into your life for the first time, the "Keepin' a Slow Profile" sections at the end of each chapter will help you to start growing in your relationship with Jesus. Find yourself a good church with some good people in it and start growing in the Lord. For more information about Jesus or if you just want to talk to someone, call **1-888-NEED-HIM** or go online to **www.needhim.org.**

Let God be your light. Keep a slow profile and your eyes on Jesus, and everything's going to be all right.

PART THREE

A LITTLE MORE ABOUT MOUNTAIN MAN

About the Author

Tim Guraedy (known as Mountain Man) lives in West Monroe, Louisiana, the small town made famous by Duck Commander and *Duck Dynasty*. Mountain Man has been a beloved character on *Duck Dynasty* since appearing in Season 1. An avid outdoorsman, he loves to hunt, fish, and daily live out his Christian faith using his time to talk with people and help those in need—all while keeping a slow profile.

Connect with Mountain Man, buy Mountain Man products, and book him for your event at

www.mountainmansworld.com

Be sure to check out and like Mountain Man's Facebook page. He presently has a weekly radio show Tuesdays at 5 p.m. Central. Speak to him LIVE by calling 800-259-1440 or 318-324-1500. Listen online at **www.TALK540.com** or watch streaming video at **new.livestream.com/KMLBradio**. His Facebook page and website will contain updated details if this information changes.

Mountain Man Favorites

Here is a list of some of my favorite things.

Saying: Emm Hmmm

Movies: *Lonesome Dove*, *Jaws*, *Rocky III*

Actors: Clint Eastwood, Robert Duvall, James Arness, Ken Curtis

Songs: "Just As I Am" (gospel hymn), "Amazing Grace," and "Who Let the Dogs Out?"

Type of music: Country

Food: Squirrel, duck eggs, a good mess of chicken and dumplings, and fried chicken

Drink: Orange soda

Candy bar: PayDay

Dessert: Banana pudding

Vehicle: Ford truck

Place to live: Anywhere in the mountains

TV shows: *Andy Griffith*, *Gunsmoke*, *The Waltons*

Historical figures: Daniel Boone, Lewis and Clark

Famous person today: Jase Robertson

President in history: Ronald Reagan

Season of the year: Fall (hunting season)

Bible verses: John 3:16–17

Book in the Old Testament: Genesis

Bible stories: Jonah and the big fish, and when Jesus multiplied the fish to feed all the people

Restaurant: LongHorn Steakhouse

Place in the USA: Hills of Tennessee

Place to travel: Alaska (I want to visit someday)

Color: Turquoise

Animal to hunt: Deer (because it's more of a challenge)

Fish to eat: Crappie (white perch)

Shot gun: Mossburg 835 Ulti-Mag (a double barrel 12-gauge sterling replica of a shotgun Teddy Roosevelt used for big game hunting)

Deer rifle: Remington automatic 5500

Lure: Rattling rogue for bass; chicken liver for catfish; beetle spin for bream (spotted bluegill)

Tool for beard maintenance: Small pair of trimming scissors to even it up and a little conditioner to keep it soft and manageable (it would feel like a scouring pad if I didn't)

Mountain Man's Ten Tips to Choose a Good Woman

You know you've found a good women when she:

1. Is sturdy enough to drag your deer out of the woods.

2. Doesn't have a beard.

3. Knows how to cook.

4. Reads her Bible.

5. Has a good truck (with a nice bass boat would be a bonus).

6. Can bait her own hook.

7. Can skin a deer.

8. Has fewer than eight pairs of shoes in her closet.

9. Doesn't mind rubbing your back.

10. Doesn't chase you around with a rolling pin when you mess up.

Acknowledgements

I'd like to thank the following people for being a part of my life:

The Lord Jesus Christ.

My parents, my sister Lynn, and brother Bill.

My son Jonathan.

Christy for giving birth to Jonathan.

The Robertson family, especially Jase for taking the time to be a messenger in the duck call room and for writing the foreword to this book.

Carl for being a good friend, hosting the radio show with me, and for being a person who leaves a clean trail.

Camilla for your kind help and assistance, and for being a computer wiz to help me out since I barely know how to turn one on.

Brian Czock who prays for me and has been a loyal friend. The Lord placed you next to me on the plane and you made the right connections for this book to happen. I can't say enough good things about you.

David Sluka for your prayers and for helping me write this book.

All the good folk at BroadStreet Publishing.

My dog Buddy for always being right there by my side.

All my fellow brothers and sisters at White's Ferry Road Church of Christ for accepting me and for all the kindness you've shown.

All my fans who have been so kind and thank me for being on a godly, moral show that their kids can watch. Thanks for your support and I hope you enjoy this book.